YOU HAVE BEEN TOLD HELL IS REAL

WHAT DOES THE BIBLE SAY?

GARRY D. PIFER

Unless otherwise noted, Scriptures are taken from the *King James Version of the Bible*, KJV.

Other Scripture quotations and references taken from the following:

Young's Literal Translation, YLT, translation made by Robert Young (1822-1888), published in 1862. In public domain.

The Bible in Basic English, BBE, a translation of the Bible into basic English by Professor S. H. Hooke. The New Testament was released in 1941 and the Old Testament in 1949, In public domain.

Weymouth New Testament, 1903 and 1912. In the public domain.

The Holy Bible, New Living Translation, NLT, Copyright © 1996, 2004, 2015 by Tyndale House Foundation. Used by permission of Tyndale House Publishers, a division of Tyndale House Ministries, Carol Stream, IL 60188. All rights reserved

Contemporary English Version, CEV, published by American Bible Society

101 N. Independence Mall, East FL 8 Philadelphia, PA 19106-2155

Holman Christian Standard Version (HCSB) New Testament copyright © 1999, whole Bible

copyright © 2004 Published by Holman Bible Publishers Nashville, TN

New International Version, NIV, Published by Biblica Used by permission.

Rotherham's Emphasized Bible, EBR, Published 1902. In public domain.

Ferrar Fenton Bible, The Holy bible in Modern Rnglish, Published 1903. In public domain.

Moffatt, New Translation, MNT, Published 1922. In public domain.

Concordant Version: The Sacred Scriptures, CVOT, CLNT, Published 1926. In public domain.

New American Standard Version, NASB, Published by Lockman Foundation. Used by permission.

New Revised Standard Version Updated Edition, NRSVUE, Copyright 2021. Published by National Council of the Churches of Christ. Used by permission.

Definitions and comments marked as follows:

Strong's Exhaustive Concordance of the Bible by James Strong, Copyright © 2009 by Thomas Nelson, Nashville, TN.

Thayer's Greek-English Lexicon of the New Testament by Joseph Henry Thayer. Copyright © 1996 by Hendrickson Publishers, Peabody, MA.

Vine's Expository Dictionary of Biblical Words by editors W. E. Vine, Merrill F. Unger, William White Jr. Copyright © 1985 by Thomas Nelson, Inc., Publishers, Nashville, TN.

The Companion Bible, Dr. E. W. Bullinger 1906-1922, Kregel Publications
2450 Oak Industrial Dr. NE
Grand Rapids, MI 49505

Interior design: www.fiverr.com freelance services
Cover design: www.fiverr.com freelance services
Proofreader/editor: Anna Hagen

Printed in the United States of America Published at Edmonton, KY
gdpifer@scrtc.com

DEDICATION

Much has transpired over the last 50 or 60 years relative to one being able to do research. If I chose to do research when in college it required a visit to the college or public library, and then one was limited by what few encyclopedias and research books were available. Thankfully we now have almost unlimited studies, dissertations, encyclopedias, and other items at our fingertips to do casual or in depth studies through the internet. My dedication of this book is to the thousands and thousands of hours that untold hundreds of individuals have devoted to providing such a wonderful resource.

CONTENTS

Introduction   1

CHAPTER ONE
Hell And the Bible   5

CHAPTER TWO
The Hebrew Word *Sheol*   9

CHAPTER THREE
Greek *Hades*   13

CHAPTER FOUR
The Greek Word *Geenna Or Gehenna*   27

CHAPTER FIVE
What Is Death, According to The Bible?   41

CHAPTER SIX
The Greek Word *Tartarus*   57

CHAPTER SEVEN
Jerome's Latin *Vulgate*   73

CHAPTER EIGHT
Dante Alighieri's Divine Comedy   77

CHAPTER NINE
John Milton's *Paradise Lost*   81

CHAPTER TEN
Did Jesus Go To Hell?   85

CHAPTER ELEVEN
Let Us Recap   97

About The Author   101

Other Books By Garry D. Pifer   103

Introduction

According to the polls conducted over the last couple of decades by the *Barna Group, Lifeway Research, Pew Research*, and by *U. S. News and World Report*, approximately 60% of Americans believe that there is a hell where certain people will be punished forever. The percentage is closer to 90% among most Protestants. However, there doesn't appear to be any one dominant view of hell. There are two popular perspectives. About 40% of those believing in hell state that it is "a state of eternal separation from God's presence." Close to one-third say that hell is "an actual place of torment and suffering where people's souls go after death." A third view held by a small percentage (13%) of adults is that "hell is just a symbol of an unknown bad outcome after death." Others were "not sure." Most of those polled did not expect to experience hell first-hand. Only about one-half of 1% believed that they would go to hell upon their death.

American poet James Whitcomb Reilly (known as the "Hoosier Poet, 1849-1916) wrote the following poem in a humorous vein.

Oh, Hell

Oh Hell—just what is meant by this word Hell.
They say sometimes it's cold as Hell,
Sometimes they say it's hot as Hell.
When it rains they say it's Hell they cry,

And it's Hell when it's dry.

They hate like Hell to see it snow,
It's a Hell of a wind when it starts to blow.
Now how in the world can anyone tell,
What in the Hell they mean by this word Hell.

This mad life is Hell they say,
When he comes in late, there's Hell to pay.
When she starts to yell it's Hell of a note,
And it's Hell when the kids you have to tote.

It's Hell when the doctor sends you his bills,
For a Hell of a lot of trips and pills.
And when you get this you will know real well,
Just what is meant by this word Hell.

Hell yes, Hell no, and oh Hell too,
The Hell you don't and the Hell you do.
And what Hell of a Hell it is,
The Hell with yours and the Hell with his.

Now where in the Hell and oh Hell where,
And what the Hell do you think I care.
But the Hell of it is sure as Hell,
That we don't know what in the Hell is Hell.

Just as Mr. Reilly says, most of us don't truly know what hell is.
We have our beliefs formed by what we have been told and taught,

perhaps by our church, our minister, by our parents, by books, by movies, and by many other means. But, have we ever done a study of the subject, or have we ever seen or read a thorough study of the subject? Does what we believe come from the Bible? Or, do these beliefs originate elsewhere? In the following pages we will investigate and come to see what hell is and what hell isn't.

I encourage you, the reader, to read with an open mind and pray that God's Spirit will give you revelation. Approach what we will be covering with a willingness to admit that you may have been given wrong information and taught things that were not true.

CHAPTER ONE

HELL AND THE BIBLE

BIBLE NOT WRITTEN IN ENGLISH

Most believers know that the Bibles we read are not in the original language, whether we read English, Spanish, German, or any other modern language. The Old Testament was written in Hebrew and that language went through many changes from the earliest books to the later ones. It is known that most of the New Testament was written in Greek, although some parts are believed to have been written in Hebrew and Aramaic. What we have available to us are translations. The first major translation was the Old Testament into Greek, which we know as the *Septuagint*. This was done by 70 (or 72) scholars. Between AD 383 and 404 Jerome translated the Bible into Latin, known as the *Vulgate*. He worked from the *Septuagint* for the Old Testament, later making some revisions working from the Hebrew scriptures. And, from the Latin, translations were later made to other languages. The best known and most used English translation was the *King James Version*, originally done in 1611.

BRITANNICA QUOTE ABOUT "HELL"

"Hell" appeared in the *King James Version* (KJV) and other early English language translations. Notice what the *Encyclopedia Britannica* says:[1]

> "The Old English *hel* belongs to a family of Germanic words meaning 'to cover' or 'to conceal.' Hel is also the name, in Old Norse, of the Scandinavian queen of the underworld. Many English language translations of the Bible use *hell* as an English equivalent of the Hebrew terms *She'ol* (or Sheol) and *Gehinnom,* or Gehnna (Hebrew *ge-hinnom*). The term Hell is also used for the Greek Hades and Tartarus, which have markedly different connotations. As this confusion of terms suggests, the idea of hell has a complex history, reflecting changing attitudes toward death and judgment, sin and salvation, and crime and punishment."

In subsequent chapters we will explore these Greek and Hebrew words.

TRANSLATIONS WITHOUT "HELL"

As mentioned above in the *Britannica* quote, many English translations, including the KJV, used "hell" for the Hebrew *sheol, gehinnom,* and the Greek *hades.* In the KJV we find the word "hell" 31 times in the Old Testament. It is most interesting to note that many, if not most, of the modern translations do not have the word "hell" at all in the Old Testament. Here are a few translations without the word

---

[1] https://www.britannica.com/topic/hell

"hell" in the Old Testament: *New International Version* (NIV), the best selling English language Bible; *New Living Translation* (NLT); *Amplified*; *New English Bible* (NET); *Holman Christian Standard Bible* (HCSB); *Young's Literal Translation* (YLT). There are many more. The word "hell" is also lacking in many New Testament translations. Here are a few: *Young's Literal Translation* (YLT); *Rotherham's Emphasized Bible* (reprinted, 1902); *Fenton's Holy Bible in Modern English* (1903); *Weymouth's New Testament in Modern Speech* (1903); *The New Testament, James Moffat* (1817); *Concordant Literal NT* (1982). And, there are many more. This absence of the word "hell" should have us questioning just what have we missed, what is wrong with what we have been taught?

CHAPTER TWO

THE HEBREW WORD *SHEOL*

SHEOL IS NOT A PLACE OF TORMENT AND SUFFERING

As mentioned earlier, the word "hell" in the KJV Old Testament (and many other English translations) was used for the Hebrew word *sheol* (Strong's number H7585). You might be surprised to know that *sheol* was used by the original authors of the Old Testament 65 times. Only 31 times did the translators use the word "hell." 30 times the KJV translators translated *sheol* as "grave." Another three times it was rendered "pit" and once as "grave's." Why would they do that? Why was there no consistency?

Notice what the *Encyclopedia Britannica* states in their article **Sheol**.[2] "**Sheol**, abode of the dead in the Hebrew Bible (the Christian Old Testament). The term can be interpreted to mean either the literal place in which dead people are placed (i.e., in the ground) or the ancient world's concept of the afterlife as a subterranean 'land of gloom and deep darkness.' Due to this ambiguity, some versions of the Bible translate Sheol as 'the grave' or 'the pit,' while other edi-

---

[2] https://www.britannica.com/topics/sacred

tions treat the word as meaning the abode of the dead." It is interesting that the writer of this piece indicates (as many others do) that the picture of a subterranean "land of gloom" was taken from the "ancient world's concepts." In other words, the ideas of various religions and thoughts of those without a knowledge and grasp of God. A bit later in the same *Britannica* article we read the following, "One notable aspect of Sheol is that many of its earliest known traits are mirrored in the concepts of the afterlife seen in the Greek Hades and the Babylonian Arallu—strongly suggesting that they are commonly derived. Also, the Jewish understanding of Sheol developed similarly to the evolution of their neighbours' beliefs about the afterlife...Considering the strong influences that the Mesopotamians and Greeks had on Jewish culture, due to their occupation of Palestine at different times, it is therefore likely that the concept of Sheol and its subsequent changes came through cultural transmission."

As we mentioned, the translators chose to use the word "hell" for some uses of *sheol* and "grave" and "pit" for others. This appears to be based only on the translator's personal belief, rather than being honest with what had been inspired. We find that there are some newer translations that are trying to be more accurate. *The New International Version* (NIV) uses the word "grave" in all but six places. Of those six, they render five as "death" and the other as "the realm of the dead." *Young's Literal Translation* (YLT), *The New American Standard Bible* (NASB), and the *New Revised Standard Version* (NRSV) are a few that use the transliteration "sheol" in all 65 places, rather than translate the word.

The question was asked on the website *quora*, "How true is it that the word hell does not exist in the original Hebrew, *Koine* Greek, and Aramaic scriptures?"[3] I believe the answer given by Dennis Cybuski, a Bible student of over 50, years is to the point. "The word "hell" is an archaic English rendition for the Hebrew word (sheol) and the Greek word (hades) that appear in the early bible writings we have today. These words rendered into modern languages would read, 'the grave or under the ground' (*sheol*), 'the place or location of the dead' (*Hades*). Nothing about a place of eternal punishment." (Note: We will look at the Greek *hades* in the next chapter.)

---

[3] https://www.quora.com/How-true-is-it-that-the-word-hell-does-not-exist-in-the-original-Hebrew-Koine-Greek-and-Aramaic-scriptures

CHAPTER THREE

GREEK *HADES*

It is impossible to give a simple answer as to the meaning of the Greek word *hades.* The word has had quite a history. Bear with us as we work our way through our study of *hades.*

HADES USED AS EQUIVALENT TO *SHEOL*

When the Old Testament was first translated into Greek (the *Septuagint*), apparently the word *hades* was used as the equivalent to the Hebrew *sheol.* As we looked at that word in the last chapter, *sheol* simply meant the grave, the pit, the unseen. Although *hades* may have originally carried that same meaning, by the time of the Old Testament translation into Greek the word had additional connotations added. The following is from the book *The Fire That Consumes* by Edward Fudge (American Christian Theologian, 7/13/44-11/25/17).[4]

"In Greek mythology Hades was the god of the underworld, then the name of the nether world itself. Charon ferried the souls of the dead across the rivers Styx or Acheron into the abode, where the watchdog Cerberus guarded the gate so none might escape. The pagan myth contained all the elements for

---

[4] The Fire That Consumes [Houston: Providential Press, 1982], pg. 205

medieval eschatology: there as the pleasant Elyusium, the gloomy and miserable Tartarus, and even the Plains of Asphodel, where ghosts could wander who were suited for neither of the above. The word hades came into biblical usage when the Septuagint translators chose it to represent the Hebrew sheol, an Old Testament concept vastly different from the pagan Greek notions just outlined. Sheol, too, received all the dead...but the Old Testament has no specific division there involving either punishment or reward."

Long before Mr. Fudge wrote the words quoted above, J. W. Hanson, D. D. wrote the book *The Bible Hell*, in 1888.[5] I'd like to share with you a few comments he makes regarding hades:

"The Hebrew Old Testament, some three hundred years before the Christian era, was translated into Greek, but of the sixty-four instances where Sheol occurs in the Hebrew, it is rendered Hadees in the Greek sixty times, so that either word is the equivalent of the other. But neither of these words is ever used in the Bible to signify punishment after death, nor should the word Hell ever be used as the rendering of Sheol or Hadees for neither word denotes post-mortem torment. According to the Old Testament the words Sheol, Hadees primarily signify only the place, or state of the dead. The character of those who departed thither did not affect their situation in Sheol, for all went into the same state. The word cannot be translated by the term

---

[5] The Bible Hell can be found at http://www.tentmaker.org/books/The Bible Hell.html

Hell, for that would make Jacob expect to go to a place of torment, and prove that the Savior of the world, David, Jonah, etc., were once sufferers in the prison-house of the damned. In every instance in the Old Testament, the word grave might be substituted for the term hell, either in a literal or figurative sense. The word being a proper name should always have been left untranslated. Had it been carried into the Greek Septuagint, and thence into English, untranslated, Sheol, a world of misconception would have been avoided, for when it is rendered Hadees, all the materialism of the heathen mythology is suggested to the mind, and when rendered Hell, the medieval monstrosities of a Christianity corrupted by heathen adulterations is suggested."

Dr. Hanson tells us that *sheol* should never have been translated as *hades* but should have been left untranslated as it was a proper name. Dr. E. W. Bullinger in Appendix 131 of *The Companion Bible* states that the rendering of *sheol*, being a proper name, when translated, it was always rendered "the grave." If **a** grave was being mentioned, the Hebrew word *qeber* or *keber* would have been used. *Qeber* is used 67 times in the Old Testament and is translated as "a grave," "graves," "a sepulcher," "sepulcher," and "a buryingplace." In the 65 times *sheol* was used, it was translated in the KJV and many other English language translations as "grave, pit, and graves" 34 times, always specified as **the** grave, **the** pit, or **the** graves. If **a** grave was being referred to it was never used with **the**.

THE GREEK LANGUAGE

Most of us are familiar with the story of the Tower of Babel. God scattered the people and confused the languages. Various languages were developed over time. Some of the earliest we know about were the Sumerian, Babylonian, and Assyrian which have come down to us on Cuneiform from ancient Mesopotamia. The ancient Egyptian languages were recorded in the Hieroglyphics. Filmmaker Timothy P. Mahoney searched for scientific evidence that Moses wrote the first books of the Bible. The compelling evidence of the development of the Hebrew language is presented in his film, *Patterns of Evidence The Moses Controversy*.[6] Hebrew was the language of the Old Testament, and it went through various stages of development. It was many years later that the Greek language was developed. There were many Greek city states, each with different dialects. Gradually a common standard, called *Koine*, meaning "common," developed. This language spread and became the most common language of the Eastern Mediterranean, primarily due to the conquests of Alexander the Great (333-323 BC). *Koine* Greek became the dominant language in politics, culture, and commerce in the whole Near East.

GREEK PHILOSOPHY

Not only the Greek language but the many beliefs and concepts of the Greek philosophers were exported to the whole area conquered by Alexander. There were many philosophers such as Socrates, Pythagoras, Heraclitus, and Homer but the one who had the most influence on later Christian thought was Plato, a student of Socrates. He lived just prior to the time of Alexander, about 428-347 BC.

---

[6] https://www.patternsofevidence.com/moses/

What are some of Plato's beliefs that found their way into Christianity? Here is a quotation from Gerhard Kittel's *Theological Dictionary of the New Testament,* Vol. VI, p. 568:

"Plato introduced into Greek philosophy the belief of the immortality of the soul and its many [re]incarnations up to the goal of final purification. According to the myth ... the soul goes to the place of judgment after leaving the body. There the judges order the righteous ... to ascend to heaven. ... The idea gradually changes from a descent of the soul to the underworld, to an ascent of the soul into heaven. The descent becomes an ascent."

Plato taught that souls lived in heaven before being born into this creation, and that they ascended back to heaven when they had sufficiently learned philosophy after a series of reincarnations. He taught that the destiny of the body was to decay into dust, but the hope of the soul was to be released from the flesh and to ascend into heaven as a pure spirit. The wicked were to descend to the underworld, designated by the Greek word *hades. Hades* took on more meaning than the unseen, the grave, or the pit. The hope of a resurrection was a totally foreign idea to Plato and the Greeks. Many writers share this information in their articles and books.

Plato wrote ten books, collectively known as *The Republic.* The concluding book was *The Myth of Er.* Unlike the way we view a myth, to the ancient Greeks it was a true story, a story that unveils the true origin of the world and human beings. Here are a couple of quotations regarding this *Myth of Er.* The first one is from an article found on the website of *Psychology Today* and is written by a psychiatrist and philosopher.[7] "Plato concluded the ten books of the *Republic* with the myth of Er, which greatly influenced the Western mind, down to our very idea of heaven and hell. Although Plato 'invented' the myth of Er, he did draw upon pre-existing elements of Greek and Egyptian mythology and cosmology." The second quotation is found in an article titled *Plato's Myths* found on the *Stanford Encyclopedia of Philosophy* website, written by Catalin Partenie, PHD.[8] "There are many myths in Plato's dialogues: traditional myths, which he sometimes modifies, as well as myths that he invents, although many of these contain mythical elements from various traditions. Plato is both a myth teller and a myth maker."

From the above quotations (and many more that can be found on the internet) it becomes quite apparent that once Plato, and others, "invented" the belief in an immortal soul they had to "figure out" what became of it after the body died. A "myth," or story, developed as to the eventual ascension of the souls of the "good people" to heaven (see a further study of this in my book *Do Christians "Go To Heaven" When They Die?*). The souls of the bad or evil people were, according to these teachings, sent to the underworld, labeled as *hades*. These false beliefs, along with the additional definitions added to the Greek word *hades,* found their way into Christian beliefs and teachings. These beliefs continued to evolve over time. Immanuel Kant (1724-1804) is considered the central figure in modern philosophy. He concluded that the soul was not demonstrable

---

[7]   https://www.psychologytoday.com/us/blog/ataraxia/202406/platos-most-beautiful-myth-retold-and-interpreted

[8] https://plato.stanford.edu/entries/plaro-myths/

through reason, but stated that the mind inevitably must reach the conclusion that the soul exists "because such a conclusion was necessary for the development of ethics and religion."

ALEXANDER'S CONTRIBUTION

Alexander the Great's military success was phenomenal but equally impressive was his advancement of Greek culture, called Hellenism. In every city Alexander conquered, he instituted schools to teach both the *Koine* Greek and Greek philosophy. Alexander was a follower of Aristotle, who was himself a student and colleague of Plato. Because of Aristotle, it appears, Alexander was positively disposed toward the Jews. He made arrangements with them that as long as they would serve him and pay their taxes they could remain autonomous. Out of gratitude to Alexander, the Jews did a number of things, one being to name every child born the next year "Alexander." By doing these things they unwittingly opened the door to the Greek language. And with the Greek language automatically came the Greek culture and the Greek philosophy. After Alexander, Judea was ruled by the Ptolemies and the Seleucids for almost two hundred years. Jewish culture and beliefs were heavily influenced by the Hellenistic culture and thought, and *Koine* Greek was used not only for international communication but also as the first language of many Jews.

GREEK IN JESUS' DAY

The languages spoken in Galilee and Judea during the time of Jesus were most likely the Semitic Aramaic and Hebrew, but Greek would have been spoken as well. It is believed that Jesus may have spoken primarily in Aramaic, but He quite likely knew and understood Hebrew and Greek. Stanley E. Porter, states in his 2004 book, "The linguistic environment of Roman Palestine during the first century was much more complex, and allows for the possibility that Jesus himself may well have spoken Greek on occasion."[9] Latin was also used by the Romans that lived and ruled there.

Even though subtle, since the Greek language was the international language even during the Roman Empire's domination of this area, Greek philosophy was becoming widely accepted. It eventually greatly affected the doctrinal teachings of Christianity.

THE GREEK NEW TESTAMENT

Most Bible scholars are in agreement that the New Testament was written in *Koine* Greek. The possible exception being the book of Matthew. Jerome, who translated much of the Bible into Latin and revised other Latin versions that were in use, (as commissioned by Pope Damasus, about 382-384 AD), states in the preface of his translation, *The Vulgate*, that Matthew published his work in Hebrew. He said, "I am now speaking of the New Testament. This was undoubtedly composed in Greek, with the exception of the work of Matthew the Apostle, who was the first to commit to writing the Gospel of Christ, and who published his work in Judaea in Hebrew characters." In recent years it has been discovered that a 14th century Spanish Jew named Shem Tov Ibn Shapeut had preserved a Hebrew version of the book of Matthew. Although his Hebrew Matthew was known for centuries, it was assumed to be simply a version from

---

[9] Porter, Stanley E. (2004). Criteria For Authenticity In Historical-jesus Research

Greek or Latin into Hebrew. In the 1980s George Howard, of Mercer University in Georgia, carried out a detailed linguistic study of this preserved version of Hebrew Matthew. He showed, after this detailed study, that there were parts of Shen Tov's Hebrew Matthew which could not be easily explained as translations from Greek. (For further details one might read the book *The Hebrew Yeshua vs. the Greek Jesus* by Nehemia Gordon[10])

As no originals exist of the New Testament books it can't be proven, but I wonder, rather than using the Greek word *hades,* perhaps the writers, being thoroughly knowledgeable of the Hebrew scriptures may have used *sheol,* knowing *sheol* was a proper noun needing no translation. In later copies the individuals doing the copying used the word *hades,* even though it contained meanings never intended by the authors. The Greek copies used by Jerome undoubtedly contained *hades.* Every place it occurred Jerome used the Latin *infernum* or the variants depending on the tenses. The Latin words have come to signify a very hot fire, an inferno. This is not the original meaning that was to be conveyed by the use of the word *sheol.* (Note: *The Latin Vulgate* became the official Bible of the Roman Catholic Church and its influence in the early Bible translations into English is very much recognized.)

Most of us have been "brought up" on the *King James Version* of the Bible. And, even the New Testament in this version only has the Greek *hades* 11 times, 10 times translated "hell." Of the 11 times

---

[10] THE HEBREW YESHUA VS. THE GREEK JESUS, Nehenia Gordon, copyright 2005, chapter 7, Hilkiah Press

hades is used we find there to be only 4 verses in the 4 gospel accounts. There is no consensus among the many translators as to the rendering in those four places. Many leave the Greek word *hades* rather than give it a translation. It is rendered "death" in some verses by some translators. In some verses there are a few translators that use the Hebrew *sheol*. Why the variations in the translations? It appears that most of the translators knew of the evolution of the Greek word *hades*. It becomes difficult to be honest with the translation and yet hold to the developed doctrine of a place of torment. (One verse of the four is found in the account of Lazarus and the rich man found in Luke 16. This story is looked at in depth in my book *THE RICH MAN AND LAZARUS – THE JEWS AND JESUS*.)

THE APOSTLE PAUL'S WRITINGS

The apostle Paul wrote approximately one-fourth of the New Testament by word count. Have we ever considered that in all of his writings he never once, not a single time, speaks about hell? If we search for the Greek word *hades* we will find 1 verse where it is used **but** it isn't translated "hell" in the KJV or in any of the other 24 or 25 translations I checked. That verse is 1 Corinthians 15:55. *The King James Version* reads "O death, where is thy sting? O grave (Greek *hades*), where is thy victory?" Paul was giving an almost exact quotation from Hosea 13:14 where *sheol* is translated "grave" two times and "death" is mentioned twice. The KJV uses the word "grave" here in 1 Cor. 15. Of the 25 versions I checked 18 use "death." 3 have it as "grave," 3 leave the Greek *hades*, and at least one has the Hebrew *sheol*. The translators knew that "hell," as commonly taught, just didn't fit. Paul speaks about death and about the resurrection, but never the "hell" we have all been taught about. We will look at some of what he presented about death and the resurrection a bit later in this book.

The apostle Paul had to contend with the Greek philosophy that heavily impacted the numerous Greek communities he went into preaching the gospel. He warned the brethren at Colosse to beware of men who would attempt to turn them from the true gospel message through philosophy, (Col. 2:8) In his letters to those living in the Greek city of Corinth he repeatedly warned them about those professing to be wise and of the wisdom of the world. Even many of the Bible commentators recognize that he was speaking out against the Greek philosophers (See 1 Cor. 1:22, 26, 30 and 1 Cor. 2:4, 5, 6. 13) We will see later that the influence became greater and has impacted the Body of Christ unto this day.

THE GREEK OLD TESTAMENT

Approximately two hundred years after Plato's teachings and thoughts came on the scene the Hebrew scriptures were translated into Greek, known as the *Septuagint*. As mentioned at the beginning of this chapter, the Greek word *hades* was apparently used where the Hebrew word *sheol* was found in the Hebrew texts. However, we can not be absolutely sure of this as the Septuagint went through a number of revisions. One source states that "the text of all print editions is derived from the recensions (revisions on the basis of critical examination of the sources) of Origen, Lucian, or Hesychius." Origen, considered an "early church father," was greatly influenced by Plato and was considered a "Christian philosopher." Lucian was referred to as a "champion of philosophy." It is questioned whether Hesychius, a Greek grammarian, was considered a Christian at all. This brings into question whether the original 70 (or 72) translators used *hades* or rather left *sheol* untranslated. Everything we have today uses the Greek *hades,* which was originally the equivalent to *sheol,* but now contains all of the additional meanings added to the word.

The Septuagint has been the basis for most translations into English and is viewed as an accurate translation, but there are detractors. *The Septuagint* has been rejected scriptural by mainstream Rabbinic Judaism. It is deemed to be different from the Hebrew source texts in many areas and appears at times to demonstrate an ignorance of Hebrew idiomatic usage. Be that as it may, it has been the basis for our English language versions of the Old Testament. And, *hades,* with all of the additional meanings and definitions, has made its way into our translations and our Christian teachings and beliefs.

GNOSTICISM

By the end of the 1st century and into the 2nd Gnosticism became quite prominent throughout the Greco-Roman world and greatly impacted the early church. What was Gnosticism? The *Encyclopedia Britannica* says of Gnosticism, "any of various related philosophical and religious movements prominent in the Greco-Roman world in the early Christian era." Later, in the same article they state the designation was applied "to the religious groups referred to in ancient sources as *gnostikoi* (Greek: 'those who have *gnosis,* or "knowledge"'). The Greek adjective *gnostikos* ('leading to knowledge' or 'pertaining to knowledge') was first used by Plato to describe the cognitive or intellectual dimension of learning, as opposed to the practical." Although there may have been a number of sources that influenced Gnosticism it seems to most that Platonism and Greek philosophy was a major source. The "big three" teachings from Plato and Greek philosophy, the immortal soul, heaven, and hell, were all being promoted and began to influence Christian teaching. The word h*ades* with all of its accumulated additional meanings was right there.

FALSE TEACHERS AND FALSE APOSTLES

We have looked at the changes in the definition and understanding of the Greek word *hades*. As we will look at later, the false teachings associated with the added connotations greatly impacted the body of believers, especially once the original apostles were no longer on the scene. However, Jesus and those original apostles and writers of the New Testament warned those they were directly dealing with, as well as leaving those warnings for us. Jesus, in verse 11 of Matthew 24, said that "many false prophets shall rise, and shall deceive many." We looked at Paul's words regarding the inroads of the Greek philosophy into the areas he was reaching. He, in almost all of his letters, gave warning as to what was going to take place. Notice a few of those warnings. In Acts 20:29-30 he was speaking to the elders of the believers in Ephesus. He pointedly told them that he knew that after his departing that "grievous wolves" would enter into their midst, and even some of those he was speaking to would speak perverse things, to draw followers after themselves. Writing to those at Rome Paul specifically told them to "mark them which cause divisions and offences contrary to the doctrine which ye have learned" (Rom. 16:17). He warned those he wrote to repeatedly about the false teachers who would enter in.

Peter also gave warning as to what would occur after his and the other apostles passing. Notice 2 Peter 2:1, "But there were false prophets also among the people, even as there shall be false teachers among you, who privily shall bring in damnable heresies, even denying the LORD that bought them, and bring upon themselves swift destruction." The apostle John wrote his gospel, letters, and the Revelation of Jesus near the end of the first century. As you read his words you will see, if you have eyes to see, the warnings he gives of what would soon occur. There would be those subverting the teachings and doctrines that came from Jesus and His apostles.

Before we look at what did occur let us look at another couple of Greeks words that have been translated into the English language as "hell." There is much yet to be covered, so stay with us.

CHAPTER FOUR

THE GREEK WORD *GEENNA* OR *GEHENNA*

JEWISH DOCTRINE OF IMMORTALITY OF THE SOUL

Judaism is believed by most, it seems, to be the absolute adherence to the words given to Moses and the covenant God made with the Israelites. Far from it. Many times over the centuries the Israelites completely got away from the "Law." They were sent into captivity at times, and there were periods of "revival." But, it is well documented that over time things were being added and others being deleted from what God had given. Repeatedly Jesus addressed the religious leaders and indicted them for "teaching for doctrine the traditions of men." By the time of Jesus, Judaism was being highly influenced by Greek philosophy, as well as other non-scriptural sources.

What developed over time appears to have begun with a belief in the "immortality of the soul" which Plato had promoted. I'd like to share with you a number of quotations.

First, from an article titled *IMMORTALITY OF THE SOUL*[11] by Kaufmann Kohler, found in the *Jewish Encyclopedia*, "The belief that the soul continues after the dissolution of the body is a matter of philosophical or theological speculation rather than simple faith, and is accordingly nowhere expressly taught in Holy Scripture." A few paragraphs further down in the article Mr. Kohler says, "The belief in the immortality of the soul came to the Jews from contact with Greek thought and chiefly through the philosophy of Plato..." Even among the various Jewish leaders there were differences of beliefs. In this same article we see a reference to this. He says, "It is not clear whether the Sadducees, in denying resurrection denied also the immortality of the soul. Certain it is that the Pharisaic belief in resurrection had not a name for the immortality of the soul." Just a couple more statements, "The immortality of martyrs was especially dwelt on by the Essenes." "This Platonic doctrine of the preexistence of the soul is taught also by the Rabbis, who spoke of the souls in the seventh heaven."

It appears that there were Jewish philosophers, just as there were Greek philosophers. As Judaism evolved these philosophers added to what was beginning in the early first century, the time of Christ. Mr. Kohler states a bit later in this article, "The medieval Jewish philosophers without exception recognized the dogmatic character of the belief in resurrection, while on the other hand they insisted on the axiomatic character of the belief in immortality of the soul." One last quotation from this article. "It was the merit of Moses Mendelssohn, the most prominent philosopher of the deistic school

---

[11] https://jewishencyclopedia.com/articles/8092-immortality-of-the-soul

in an era of enlightenment and skepticism, to have revived by his 'Phaedon' the Platonic doctrine of immortality, and to have asserted the divine nature of man by presenting new arguments in behalf of the spiritual substance of the soul. Thenceforth Judaism, and especially progressive or Reform Judaism emphasized the doctrine of immortality." A couple of sentences later he states, "Immortality of the soul, instead of resurrection, was found to be 'an integral part of the Jewish creed'..."

JEWISH *GE-HINNOM*

Once a belief in the immortality of the soul was arrived at, a teaching had to be developed, much as had been done by Plato and other Greek philosophers, as to where these souls went following death. A brief statement regarding the belief that was established is found in a short article titled *Gehinnom: A Jewish Hell*, found on the *myjewishlearning* website.[12] "Only truly righteous souls ascend directly to the Garden of Eden, say the sages. The average person descends to a place of punishment and/or purification, generally referred to as *Gehinnom*. The name is taken from a valley (*Gei Hinnom*) just south of Jerusalem, once used for child sacrifice by the pagan nations of Canaan (II Kings 23:10). Some view *Gehinnom* as a place of torture and punishment, fire and brimstone. Others imagine it less harshly, as a place where one reviews the actions of his/her life and repents for past misdeeds."

---

[12]   https://www.myjewishlearning.com/article/heaven-and-hell-in-jewish-tradition/

Rabbi Baruch HaLevi, writing for the *JewishBoston* website[13] makes the following statements. "Yes, Judaism believes in 'heaven,' and yes, Judaism also believes in 'hell.' Again, there is no one depiction of the world on high, so too 'the world below' is equally nuanced, sophisticated and diverse in description. The Torah refers to a place called '*Sheol*,' originally a physical location and later a spiritual destination for sinners and troubled souls. Some, particularly the Kabbalists, viewed *Sheol* as a necessary stopping point for all souls on their journey from this world to the next, a place to work through the sins of this life. Later, the Jewish mystical tradition expanded upon this notion, describing an even more complex version called '*Gehinnom*.'"

Before moving on I'd like you to notice with me the numerous words and phrases used by the various writers we quoted. Here are a few, "philosophical or theological speculation," "Platonic doctrine," "Jewish philosophers," "Kabbalists," and "Jewish mystical tradition," not scriptural or biblical doctrine, but the vain reasoning of men.

NEW TESTAMENT USAGE OF *GEHENNA*

The word *gehenna,* rendered most often "hell" in our English language bibles, occurs 12 times, 11 times in the gospels and once in the book of James. *Gehenna* is a transliteration of *Ge-Hinnom* in Hebrew, the Valley of Hinnom, a deep, narrow glen to the south of Jerusalem, where, after the introduction of the worship of the fire-gods by Ahaz, the idolatrous Jews sacrificed their children to Molech,

---

13 https://www.jewishboston.com/read/ive-always-read-that-jews-don't-believe-in-the-concept-of-hell-is-that-true/

30

(2 Kings 23:10). At the time of Jesus it was a place where all kinds of refuse was burned, much like "city dumps" used to be here in the United States before laws were enacted that required everything to be covered with earth, known now as landfills.

The 11 times the word *Gehenna* is used in the gospels it was spoken by Jesus. We need to understand what He was saying. Was He speaking of a place of "eternal torment" of immortal souls? **No!** As we quoted earlier from an article by Kaufmann Kohler, "The belief that the soul continues its existence after the dissolution of the body is a matter of philosophical or theological speculation rather than of simple faith, and is accordingly nowhere expressly taught in Holy Scripture."[14] (We will look at Jesus' view and teaching about death a bit later.) As was pointed out earlier, the doctrine of *Gehinnom* evolved within Judaism over time. At the time of Jesus, in the early 1st century, the basic idea was of "the place of spiritual punishment and/or purification for the wicked dead."[15] Jesus used the same term Rabbinical Judaism was using, *Gehinnom*, using the physical fire and burning in the Valley of Hinnom to speak of a spiritual process of purification. Much of what Jesus was teaching His disciples has been terribly misunderstood.

(The passages where Jesus used the word *Gehinnom*, or Greek *Geenna*, are Matt. 5:22, 29, 30, Matt. 10:28, Matt. 18:9, Matt. 23:15, 33, Mark 9:43, 45, 47, and Luke 12:5. The verses in Mark are a parallel of Matt. 5.)

---

[14] https://jewishencyclopedia.com/articles/8092-immortality-of-the-soul
[15] Judaism 101 http://www.jewfaq.org/cgi-bin/search.cgi?Keywords=hell

In about one-half of those passages Jesus adds "fire" to His use of *Gehinnom*. I believe it is very important to look at the word "fire."

FIRE IN THE BIBLE

Few of us associate the word "fire" with the Creator Himself. We generally think of destruction such as Sodom and Gomorrah. However, the attributes of "light" and "heat" from fire speak more of the Creator and His goodness than of a destructive force against His enemies. The writers of the Bible employed the use of "fire" in many different ways. A study of these many ways can be extremely fascinating. We will refer to only a few here. One of the first examples we find is in the covenant God made with Abraham in Genesis 15:17. *The King James Version* has "a smoking furnace," and a "burning lamp." Other translations have it as "a flaming torch" and "a blazing torch." God appeared to Moses in a burning bush. During the exodus from Egypt, God was in the pillar of fire. When the covenant was made with Israel at Mt. Sinai God came down in fire and smoke. In Psalms 104:4 it states that God's ministers are "a flaming fire." Even God's Holy Spirit is likened to fire. When it was first given on Pentecost we are told that there "appeared unto them cloven tongues like as of fire" (Acts 2:3).

We most often think of fire as destroying things. We may say things like, "His home was destroyed by fire." We understand what is meant, but what has actually occurred is the components of the house have been changed. The various elements in the wood, for example, have changed forms. Let me try to make this simple. I burn firewood in my stove to heat our home. Combustion is the process by which the elements within the piece of firewood change form.

When wood is burned, the heat causes the chemicals from which the wood is composed to vaporize, mixing with the oxygen in the air to form new chemicals, including water and the gas carbon dioxide. Minerals remain as ashes. What was formerly a tree is no longer in the form of a tree, but the substance thereof is simply **changed** into a **different form** and exists in its new form. The change is not just a physical change but a chemical change. Thus, to burn means to **change**.

Fire changes things. A major change a fire makes is that it PURIFIES. Most of us don't realize that many of our English words speak of this. The Greek word translated "fire" in the New Testament is *pur* (pronounced poor), Strong's Number G4442. This Greek word is the root of many of our English words: **pur**e, **pur**ity, **pur**ify, **pur**ge, **pur**ification. The basic thread is that of purifying. The Hebrew word for fire has much the same meaning. A prophetic passage we should look at is found in the book of Malachi, chapter 3: 1-3:

"Behold, I will send my messenger, and he shall prepare the way for me: and the LORD, whom ye seek, shall suddenly come to his temple, even the messenger of the covenant, whom ye delight in: behold, he shall come, saith the LORD of hosts. But who may abide the day of his coming? and who shall stand when he appeareth? for he is like a refiner's fire, and like fullers' soap: and he shall sit as a refiner and purifier of silver: and he shall purify the sons of Levi, and purge them as gold and silver, that they may offer unto the LORD an offering in righteousness."

In addition to speaking of "fire" Jesus also mentions in a few of the passages that the fire "never shall be quenched." Was He speaking of fire that would burn for all "eternity" and never stop burning? Let us look at what He was saying.

UNQUENCHABLE FIRE

The statement Jesus made about "fire that never shall be quenched" is a simple statement to understand if we don't twist what "quench" means. Originally the word meant "to extinguish fire." Today it has been expanded somewhat to include putting an end to something or to satisfy. Jesus was saying this purifying fire, pictured by the fires burning in *Gehinnom,* would not be extinguished or put out by pouring water on the flames. However, this fire He was speaking of would quit burning when all the fuel was consumed. He was **not** indicating that it would burn for "eternity" as it has been falsely explained.

In making this statement Jesus was quoting from Isaiah 66:24, a verse that His disciples knew. So did most of the multitude that was hearing Him. This verse in Isaiah 66 also mentions "their worm shall not die" and Jesus quotes that as well (Mark 9:44, 46, and 48). What is that all about? Immortal worms?

THEIR WORM DIETH NOT

If Jesus had been speaking of the "hell" most have been told about, we have a bit of a dilemma in understanding what kind of worms never die (Mark 9:44, 46, and 48). Are there "immortal" worms? Or, are there worms that can withstand the fire? What was He saying? A simple little bit of research answers those questions. Strong's definitions says, "a grub, maggot, or earth worm." Thayer's speaks of these worms as "worms, specifically that kind which preys upon dead bodies." Hopefully we begin to understand. Flies of various types lay their eggs in rotting flesh, discarded food scraps, and other types of refuse. The natural process is for the eggs to hatch into "maggots," sometimes referred to as worms. Depending on temperature and other conditions this takes only a few hours. Within just a few days the maggots go through their metamorphasis and turn into flies. They never die (at least naturally) but are simply the larva stage of flies. These maggots feed upon the material until they make this change. They are never burned up in the fire but live in the refuse that would be on the outside edges of the "garbage dump."

THE LAKE OF FIRE

There are five verses found in the book of Revelation that speak of a "lake of fire." Most theologians and believers see this as being the same as the Jewish *Gehenna*. Let us take a brief look:

Rev. 19:20, "And the beast was taken, and with him the false prophet that wrought miracles before him, with which he deceived them that had received the mark of the beast, and them that worshipped his image. These both were cast alive into a lake of fire burning with brimstone."

Rev. 20:10, "And the devil that deceived them was cast into the lake of fire and brimstone, where the beast and false prophet are, and shall be tormented day and night for ever and ever."

Rev. 20:14, "And death and hell were cast into the lake of fire. This is the second death."

Rev. 20:15, "And whosoever was not written in the book of life was cast into the lake of fire."

Rev. 21:8, "But the fearful, and unbelieving, and the abominable, and murderers, and whoremongers, and sorcerers, and idolaters, and all liars, shall have their part in the lake which burneth with fire and brimstone: which is the second death."

One thing these verses have in common is that they are all from the book of Revelation. In listening to the numerous individuals who quote and teach from this book, one thing that becomes apparent is that many take some passages as literal and other passages as merely symbolic. It seems that the individual chooses which way to view them based on their own personal view. But, one needs only to look to the first verse of the first chapter of the book to determine how to look at what we are given. Revelation 1:1, "The Revelation of Jesus Christ, which God gave unto him, to shew unto his servants things which must shortly come to pass; and he sent and **signified** it by his angel unto his servant John." Did you catch that? I emphasized the word "signified" by putting it in bold characters. What does the word mean? Look at the following.

Strong's definition says "to indicate." Vine's Dictionary of Biblical Words states under the definition for the Greek word *semaino,* Strong's number G4591, "Where perhaps the suggestion is that of expressing by signs." I especially like what Albert Barnes tells us in his commentary of this verse. "He indicated it by signs and symbols." He then continues, "It properly refers to some sign, signal, or token by which anything is made known, and is a word most happily chosen to denote the manner in which the events referred to were to be communicated to John, for nearly the whole book is made up of signs and symbols." We need to be very careful in attaching a literal meaning to verses that are using a symbol.

It should be clear to us that the "fire" being depicted is likened to literal fire but is of a spiritual nature. Remember we are looking at a sign or symbol. We just looked at the passage in Malachi which speaks of purifying and purging the sons of Levi. This is the "fire of God." Let us notice a few things that substantiate this. In Luke 3:16 John the Baptist, speaking of Jesus, says, "He shall baptize you with the Holy Ghost and with fire." The word translated "and" is the Greek word *kai*, Strong's number G2532. It is most often translated "and," however other accurate translations are "also, even, indeed, but." It is translated "even" over 500 times in the New Testament. What John was stating is that the Holy Ghost, or Holy Spirit, is a spiritual fire.

Looking at the five verses which speak of the "lake of fire" we find three of them also include "brimstone." The Greek word is *theion*, Strong's number G2303. Strong's definition is "sulphur." Thayer's adds "divine incense." Vine's says "originally denoted 'fire from heaven.'" Charles Pridgeon (president and founder of the *Pittsburgh Bible Institute*, 1863-1932) comments about "brimstone" and refers to the *Liddell and Scott Greek-English Lexicon*, 1897 Edition.[16] He says, "The word *theion* translated 'brimstone' is exactly the same word *theion* which means 'divine.' Sulfur was sacred to the deity among the ancient Greeks and was used to fumigate, to purify, and to cleanse and to consecrate to the deity." He continues a bit

---

[16] Charles Pridgeon, Is Hell Eternal? Or Will God's Plan Fail? Chapter Eleven

further on, "The verb derived from *theion* is *theioo*, which means to hallow, to make divine, or to dedicate to a god." It is here that he refers to Liddell and Scott. Mr. Pridgeon then comments, "To any Greek, or to any trained in the Greek language, a 'lake of fire and brimstone' would mean a 'lake of divine purification.'"

The apostle Paul also speaks of this fire, the fire of God. We won't quote the entire passage but just a couple of verses from 1 Corinthians chapter 3. Speaking about our foundation being Jesus Christ, he speaks of men building with gold, silver, precious stones, wood, hay, and stubble. Let us pick up his words in verses 13-15, "Every man's work shall be made manifest: for the day shall declare it, because it shall be revealed by fire; and the fire shall try every man's work of what sort it is. If any man's work abide which he hath built thereupon, he shall receive a reward. If any man's work shall be burned, he shall suffer loss; but he himself shall be saved; yet so as by fire."

Can we understand what John is telling us in these five verses about "the lake of fire and brimstone"? Those individuals "cast" into the "lake" will have the purifying divine fire of God working upon them to burn up the **works** built with "wood, hay, and stubble." The "lake of fire" is not to burn up, nor destroy, nor torment these individuals for all eternity. "But wait" some of you may be saying. "Revelation 20:10 says, that they 'shall be tormented day and night for ever and ever." Yes, that is what the *King James Version* says. Once again the translation is the issue. The Greek word translated "ever" (2 times) is *aion*, Strong's number G165. Strong's definition is "properly an age." Vine's also says "an age." Among a number that translate this passage as "ages of the ages" are *Literal Translation of* *the Bible, Weymouth New Testament*, and *Young's Literal Translation*. The time that this purifying takes may be quite some length of time, but it ends when the purifying has been accomplished by the action of the Divine Fire of God.

*V*erse 12 of Revelation 20 tells us of the dead, small and great, and the judgment that will be upon them. As we continue reading we are told that "death and hell" delivered up the dead. "Hell" simply means the grave. Verse 14 has a statement that has been the basis of much doctrinal debate, "This is the second death." This phrase answers the first part of the verse, "And death and hell were cast into the lake of fire." When the work of the Divine Fire is done there will no longer be any death or any graves. Their ending is "the death of death." We were told in 1 Corinthians 15, the resurrection chapter, verse 26, "The last enemy that shall be destroyed is death."

Earlier we saw that the belief and teaching regarding individuals being cast into "*Gehenna* fire" for "eternal torment" was based on a belief in an immortal soul. I mentioned that we would look at what Jesus and the rest of the Bible has to say about what death is. So, we will devote the next chapter to look at what death is and what that is all about. (For additional information and understanding regarding an immortal soul please obtain and read my book *WHAT DOES THE BIBLE SAY ABOUT AN IMMORTAL SOUL?*)

CHAPTER FIVE

What Is Death, According to The Bible?

Do a quick Google search on the internet and you will find scores of definitions and ideas concerning death. Some things advanced are from a "scientific" view. Some thoughts are from political opinion. And, you will find many thoughts and opinions put forth by numerous Bible teachers and believers. Even those ideas vary. Here is a sampling:

"Death, dying, and the afterlife are all shrouded in deep mystery, cloaked in darkness and generally surrounded by fear and apprehension. The very idea of death strikes fear into many people's hearts."

"Death is the cessation of the connection between our mind and our body. Most people believe that death takes place when the heart stops beating; but this does not mean that the person has died, because his subtle mind may still remain in his body."

"Death may be the most misunderstood subject in the world today."

"Death, the total cessation of life processes that eventually occurs in all living organisms. The state of human death has always been obscured by mystery and superstition, and its precise definition remains controversial, differing according to culture and legal systems."

"Although there is no universally accepted definition of death, a 1971 Kansas statute comes close: 'A person will be considered medically and legally dead if, in the opinion of a physician, based on ordinary standard of medical practice, there is absence of spontaneous brain function.'"

Let us view a few of the thoughts and opinions of some Bible teachers and believers:

"Death is inevitable to whatever is born. The Soul is free from the bondage of birth and death. It is eternal; it has no death. Anything that is born has to die, and because there is death, there will also be birth. So death is connected to birth. Wherever there is birth there is death."

"According to the Bible, death is not the end of life but the separation of the soul from the body. Scripture clearly speaks of both eternal life with God in heaven and eternal separation from God in hell."

"The Biblical definition of death - whether physical or spiritual - is not non-existence, but separation."

"Physical death is the separation of body and soul."

There is apparently no universal agreement on the subject of death. There are many opinions, beliefs and thoughts. But, is there an authoritative source where we can get some answers? Yes, thankfully there is. We are going to see what the Bible says by looking first at what Jesus taught. He was God in the flesh, by whom all things were created. He is the one who created and set in motion life and death. He, I believe, knows whereof He speaks.

JESUS' TEACHING

We will begin by looking at His words in John 11 and 12. You are familiar with the story of Jesus' friend Lazarus being raised from the dead by Jesus. There is *so-o-o* much in this account and we won't be able to cover every bit of what is there, but we will look at what Jesus has to say about death.

Beginning in the first verse of chapter 11, John gives us a bit of the back story. Martha, Mary, and Lazarus were friends of Jesus. John, in verse 2, recounts the event of Mary anointing the feet of Jesus with ointment and wiping His feet with her hair. John gets right to the heart of the story by telling us that Lazarus was sick. This was a very serious illness, and the sisters sent a messenger to Jesus informing Him. All indications are that Jesus was at Bethabara, beyond the Jordan, approximately 20 miles away from Bethany, perhaps a day's journey for the messenger. (See John 1:28 and John 10:40.)

In verse four we read Jesus' response, which was most likely carried back to Martha and Mary by the messenger. There has been much discussion over what Jesus said. Our English *King James Version* renders His words thus, "This sickness is not unto death, but for the glory of God, that the Son of God might be glorified thereby."

We have the benefit of the rest of the story that John gives us and can gain understanding. Those standing there at the time, including Jesus' disciples, missed what He was saying. He knew by a Word of Knowledge, that at the moment He was speaking, Lazarus had already died. The text tells us that word came to Him of Lazarus' sickness which, as we mentioned above, it would have taken a day for the messenger to arrive. In verse 6 we are told that Jesus remained where He was for two days. After this He and His disciples made the trip to Bethany, a full day's journey. When they arrived, we are told in verse 17, He found that Lazarus "had lain in the grave four days already."

So, what was Jesus expressing in verse four? What did He mean, "This sickness is not unto death," when He was aware that Lazarus was already in the grave? Knowing what we do from John's account we could possibly state it more clearly. Jesus could have as well, but He wanted His words to be a bit cryptic, keeping the meaning hidden and concealed.

Maybe it will be a bit clearer if we word it differently. For example, "Death, resulting from this sickness, is not the last word!" "Although this sickness may bring death, that is not the conclusion to this situation." "Lazarus' sickness will result in great glory to God. He may die but it won't hold him." "This sickness will not end in a death lasting until the great resurrection of all, but will be one to bring glory to God and to His Son."

After making this statement, John tells us a couple of things that are important to the story. He tells us in verse five that Jesus loved Martha, Mary and Lazarus. He had a very special connection with them. Now, John tells us that when Jesus got the message that Lazarus was sick, He didn't go rushing off to Bethany, **but** He "abode two days still in the same place where He was." Now, as we rehearsed above, Jesus was fully aware of the situation and knew what He was doing.

Then, in verse seven, Jesus said to His disciples, "Let us go into Judea again." He didn't make mention here of Lazarus. And, His disciples responded, saying in essence, "What are you thinking? The Jews recently were seeking you to kill you, and you want to go back there?"

We won't try to go into His whole response, given in verses 9 and 10, but let us look at verse 11. Notice His words, "Our friend Lazarus sleepeth; but I go, that I may awake him out of sleep." When the disciples heard this they said, and I paraphrase, "Hey, if he is asleep he'll be fine." John then explains, verse 13. "Howbeit Jesus spake of his death: but they thought that He had spoken of taking rest in sleep." Then Jesus said unto them plainly, "Lazarus is dead" (verse 14).

DEATH AND SLEEP

Did we catch what Jesus says? He equates death with sleeping. And, this was not a new concept to those there with Him. In the Old Testament scriptures we find this expressed over and over. In fact we find an interesting expression mentioned in connection with various individuals, "slept with his fathers." This expression is used over 35 times and is clearly speaking of death. Let us look at one account, 1 Kings 2:10, "So David slept with his fathers, and was buried in the city of David." One isn't buried if he is taking a rest. As we read earlier, when Jesus said He was going to awake Lazarus from sleep, His disciples thought He was referencing "taking of rest in sleep." Jesus had to make it quite clear that He was speaking of death, verse 14 of John 11, "Lazarus is dead."

Jesus says two things, with the same meaning. "Lazarus sleepeth;..." and "Lazarus is dead." This study won't get into all the scientific research into sleep but I believe we all know what sleep is. We sleep every night (or day) and we may not know all that research goes into, but we know the basics. We sleep. We are unaware of anything happening around us. We are unaware of the passage of time. We look at a clock and mentally calculate how long we slept. I'd like to quote from a short article I found on the internet concerning sleep.[17] "In other words, a sleeping person is unconscious to most things happening in the environment." A bit later in the same article, "a sleeping person can be aroused if the stimulus is strong enough." It is stated that not only man but reptiles, birds and mammals all sleep. And quoting again, "That is, they become unconscious to their surroundings for periods of time."

OLD TESTAMENT WRITERS

When we are asleep we are unaware of what is taking place around us. We are unconscious to what is happening. Jesus is affirming what was known and understood by the writers of the Old Testament and by those around Him at the time, sleep is a shadow of death. Solomon, the wisest man who ever lived, knew and understood sleep and

---

[17] https://tinyurl.com/4p96p3x2

death. Notice what he writes in Ecc. 9:5, "For the living know that they shall die: but the dead know not any thing,..." Just as in sleep, we are unconscious, not knowing anything that is happening around us. When we are dead, we do not know anything. David, Solomon's father, also knew this truth. In Psalms 146 and verse four he writes, "His breath goeth forth, he returneth to the earth; in that very day his thoughts perish."

Back a few pages we read another verse that David penned expressing much the same thing. Psa. 115:16, "The dead praise not the Lord, neither any that go down into silence." Earlier in the Psalms David makes another statement along the same line. Psa. 6 and verse five he is in context speaking to God and says, "For in death there is no remembrance of thee: in the grave who shall give thee thanks?" No, the dead have no memory, no thoughts, and are not praising God and giving Him thanks. They are "asleep!"

Isaiah, the prophet, tells us the same things we read from Solomon and David. Notice Isa. 38:18-19, "For the grave cannot praise thee, death can not celebrate thee: they that go down into the pit cannot hope for thy truth. The living, the living, he shall praise thee, as I do this day:..." Plainly it is only the living that are able to praise God. The dead are asleep, unconscious, to any and everything. They are not able to praise and celebrate God. Their thoughts have perished.

Job, who lived long before David, Solomon or Isaiah, understood about death. Let us look at what he expressed while he was going through his trial. In chapter 14 of Job we read, beginning with verse 10 and through verse 14:

"But man dieth, and wasteth away: yea, man giveth up the ghost, and where is he? As the waters fail from the sea, and the flood decayeth and drieth up: So man lieth down, and riseth not: till the heavens be no more, they shall not awake, nor be raised out of their sleep. O that thou wouldest hide me in the grave, that thou wouldest keep me in secret, until thy wrath be past, that thou wouldest appoint me a set time, and remember me! If a man die, shall he live again? All the days of my appointed time will I wait, till my change come."

Did you notice that Job knew and understood that death was equated to being asleep. Look again at the words he used. "But man dieth, and wasteth away;" "So man lieth down, and riseth not:" "they shall not awake, nor be raised out of their sleep." "All the days of my appointed time will I wait, till my change come." Yes, he knew that in death he would be asleep awaiting a resurrection.

Daniel also speaks of death as sleep, Dan. 12:2. The prophet Jeremiah speaks in the 51st chapter of Jeremiah about those who sleep a perpetual sleep. Brown, Driver, Briggs Concordance gives as the first definition of the word perpetual, "long duration." But, all of these men of God also knew and spoke of a time of awakening from the sleep of death, of a resurrection.

RESURRECTION

The resurrection was paramount in Jesus' miracle and teaching about death and sleep in John 11. When Jesus spoke to Martha as He came into Bethany, He told her that her brother would "rise again," verse 23. Martha believed in the resurrection of the dead and responded that she knew that Lazarus would rise again at the last day, verse 24. But, Jesus made His point, verse 25, "I am the resurrection..." He knew what He was going to do in just a short time.

As I said earlier, there is so much in this account. Jesus taught about death, but, He also taught about resurrection. And, in all of this we also understand that He was showing that He would soon die, be put into the grave, and would be resurrected. Let us notice again what He says about Lazarus.

In verse 39 of John 11 we find Jesus at the grave, and He speaks to Martha. Look at how this verse refers to her, "Martha, the sister of him that was dead." Lazarus was dead. He had earlier said that Lazarus was asleep. In verse 44 of John 11, after Jesus called for Lazarus to come forth, we read that "he that was dead came forth." Continuing the story in chapter 12 we are told that six days before the passover Jesus came to Bethany "where Lazarus was which had been dead, whom he raised from the dead." The resurrection of Lazarus, the raising him from the dead was, as Jesus had said in verse 11 of chapter 11, the act of awakening him out of sleep.

We have read what Jesus said, and what many of the Old Testament prophets and writers have written equating death with sleep. Let us now notice what is written and recorded by Paul and other New Testament writers.

Luke wrote both the gospel of Luke and the book of Acts. In chapter 13 of the book of Acts, verse 36, he speaks of King David. "For David, after he had served his own generation by the will of God fell on sleep, and was laid unto his fathers, and saw corruption." Slightly different wording but exactly what we read earlier, "David slept with his fathers and was buried."

The apostle Paul gave us a great amount of teaching on death and the resurrection. We'll look at a few passages. In his discussion of eating of the bread and taking of the cup in 1 Cor. 11:30, what has been called communion, he speaks of those who eat and drink without proper discernment of the Lord's body. He says, "For this cause many are weak and sickly among you, and many sleep." His reference to sleep is indicating that many had died when they should have been receiving healing.

We'll turn to the 15th chapter of 1 Corinthians in a moment, to what is referred to as "the resurrection chapter" but let us first look at Paul's words in 1 Thes. 4. Beginning with verse 13, "But I would not have you to be ignorant, brethren, concerning them which are asleep." As we continue reading it becomes quite clear that he is speaking of those who have died, not just taking rest. Verse 14, "For if we believe that Jesus died and rose again, even them which sleep in Jesus." Let us continue, verse 15, "...that we which are alive and remain unto the coming of the Lord shall not prevent them which are asleep." He repeatedly calls death sleep. Now, we come to verse 16 where Paul makes it very clear that the sleep he has been speaking of is death. "...and the dead in Christ shall rise first." (I didn't quote every word Paul wrote here as there would be a dozen studies or sermons generated.)

Now, to 1 Cor. 15. Once again, there is so much that could be covered, but we'll look specifically at his statements correlating sleep and death. He begins teaching about death and the resurrection in verse 12, speaking of Jesus rising from the dead. Let us drop down to verse 18, "Then they also which are fallen asleep in Christ..." Verse 20, "...and become the firstfruits of them that slept." We know that his references to sleep are equated to death, as he continues in the following verses. Verse 21, "For since by man came death, by man came also the resurrection of the dead." Verse 22, "For as in Adam all die,..." And verse 26, "The last enemy that shall be destroyed is death."

Going down to verse 51, Paul tells us, "Behold, I shew you a mystery; We shall not all sleep, but we shall all be changed." Verse 52 says, "and the dead shall be raised incorruptible, and we shall be changed." Then in verse 55 we read, "O death, where is thy sting? O grave, where is thy victory?"

From one end of the Bible to the other, the words and teachings of Jesus are repeated by the writers of scripture, death is over and over again referred to as sleep, an unconscious state, in which one is unaware of what is going on around them. Thoughts have perished. It is a period of awaiting being "awakened" at the resurrection.

I know that "religion," has told us much that is contrary to what we have been reading. I hear many, without scriptural support, state that when a person dies he has "gone home," or has "gone to heaven," or is now "with Jesus." One individual that I have learned a lot from and come to appreciate recently made a statement on a live-streamed study, that David had gone to heaven and was with Jesus. I wanted to shout out through the internet, "That isn't what Scripture says!" Let us read what the Bible tells us about David in Acts 2:29, which is part of Peter's message on the Day of Pentecost, "Men and brethren, let me freely speak unto you of the patriarch David, that he is both dead and buried, and his sepulcher is with us unto this day." He says David is dead (asleep) and is buried. But, wait! Let us read further. Notice, please, verse 34, "For David is not ascended into the heavens:" This is plain and tells us exactly what we have been reading. David, along with all who have died, has fallen asleep, and is sleeping in his grave awaiting the resurrection, waiting to be awakened.

SPIRIT, SOUL, AND BODY

I know some of you are thinking and saying, "But don't the soul and spirit leave and go to God?" We read some of Solomon's statements earlier concerning death, and he also makes a statement regarding this question. In Ecc. 12:7 we read, "Then shall the dust return to the earth as it was: and the spirit shall return unto God who gave it." Is he saying, as many teach, that the spirit goes to heaven and is dwelling with God and all the saved who have died? How does that fit with the numerous scriptures we have just read about "sleeping" in the graves until the resurrection? Let us look at something else that Solomon said, Ecc. 3:21. "Who knoweth the spirit of man that goeth upward, and the spirit of the beast that goeth downward to the earth?" A few other translations make this question a bit clearer. Let us look at a few. The *Bible in Basic English* says, "Who is certain that the spirit of the sons of men goes up to heaven...?" The *Contemporary English Version* has, "Who really knows if our spirits go up and the spirits of animals go down into the earth?" The *New Living Translation* renders this verse as, "For who can prove that the human spirit goes up...?"

Solomon, who was the wisest man who ever lived because of God's great gift, understood that the breath and the spirit left the body at death, that it "returned to God," **but** he didn't know and he asked how any knew just where it went — did it go up to heaven?

There is no revelation on that. We know that it goes to God for safe keeping until the resurrection.

One of the greatest revelations we have came from the Apostle Paul. It is recorded for us in 1 Thes. 5:23, "And the very God of peace sanctify you wholly; and I pray God your whole spirit and soul and body be preserved blameless unto the coming of our Lord Jesus Christ." Several translations make this a bit clearer by stating "your whole being–spirit, soul and body." *Thayer's Greek Definitions* defines the Greek word, *holokleros*, Strong's G3648, here translated 'whole,' as "complete in all its parts, in no part wanting or unsound, complete, entire, whole." Without all three components we are not a "whole being." Although not a perfect analogy, it is true that your car is not whole if you just have the body but no engine and transmission. You might have an engine and transmission, but without a body to put them into you don't have a car.

We can get a bit of the picture of what death is like, again, from the reference to sleep. When we are asleep, the body is in a bit of a slowed down, suspended state. The soul and spirit, where our thinking, our emotions, etc. are located, also are inactive. When we are sound asleep we are not thinking, planning, or expressing emotions. The instant we wake up we may immediately recall what we were thinking before we "fell asleep." If we were sad, happy, etc. our emotions come back immediately. But, during sleep, as during the time we are dead, there are no thoughts, we are not praising God or cursing anyone.

DEAD IN CHRIST

There are so many related studies that cry out to be done after reading many of these passages, but they don't fall under the scope of this study. Let's just look at a few more verses. We read much of what Paul wrote in 1 Cor. 15. Let us review a few things before we turn to our final verses. Paul stated in verse 22 that in Adam all die and even so, in like accord, in Christ shall all be made alive. Note, the dead aren't alive. In verse 23 he tells us that all will be made alive "in his own order." And he gives us a bit of that order, Christ the firstfruits, afterward they that are Christ's at his coming. Paul tells us plainly who these are over in 1 Thes. 4:14, "them also which sleep in Jesus." In verse 15 he refers to them as "them which are asleep." Verse 16 he again refers to the "dead in Christ" rising first.

Okay, let us turn to our final passage over in the book of Revelation. Let's read chapter 20 though we won't attempt to explain all that is there in this study. In verses 1-5 John speaks of the devil being bound and then of seeing thrones and those sitting on them being given judgment. He describes those who hadn't come under the deception of the adversary. He tells us that these would live and reign with Christ a thousand years. And, in verse 5 we are told that the rest of the dead didn't live again until after the thousand years. Then he tells us what he has just written about is the first resurrection, the resurrection of those that Paul called the dead in Christ, those that "sleep in Jesus."

John, here in Revelation 20, tells us about those that are a part of the first resurrection, verse 6, and of the devil being loosed for a short period after the thousand years. Now, to the verses that are most pertinent to our study. Verse 11 speaks of a great white throne and then in verse 12 he sees "the dead, small and great, stand before God." This, in light of verse 5, is the rest of the dead, those who were not the dead in Christ, those who did not sleep in Jesus. Note, he says they were the dead. Verse 13 says they were resurrected from the sea and "death and hell delivered up the dead." Verse 14 also speaks of "death and hell." There are all kinds of teachings about this, but simply put he is saying "those that are in the grave," be it a watery grave or anywhere they may have been buried.

Judgment, the casting of death and hell into the lake of fire, can be discussed at another time. But, the point for now is that all of these were dead, and they were raised to life to stand before God. They were resurrected, not at Jesus' return when the "dead in Christ," those that were "asleep in Jesus," were resurrected, but in their order, as John said, after the thousand years.

This was not "spirit and soul" coming from heaven to be put back into a body and then to enter a period of judgment. A common teaching presumes that there has been a judgment at death for them to have been "sent upward or downward." No, based on all the numerous scriptures we have looked at, when they died they were asleep, unconscious awaiting this moment being described, being delivered from the sea and their graves. All the dead, not in Christ, small and great, young and old, from all time periods, each "in his own order" will awake from this sleep of death to stand before God.

Although there is *so-o-o* much more we could look at, I believe the scriptures we have looked at tell us plainly that death is pictured

by sleep. It isn't something unfathomable, something all that difficult to understand. Sure, there are aspects we may not totally grasp
but we don't have to be confused by the many and varied teachings
given by religion.

CHAPTER SIX

THE GREEK WORD *TARTARUS*

We have looked at the Hebrew word *sheol* and the Greek words *hades* and *gehenna*, translated as "hell" in most of our English language Bibles. There is one more Greek word that we need to examine, the Greek word *tartaroo* or *tartaro*, which we are told is derived from *tartarus*. This Greek word appears only once in the New Testament and is almost always translated as "hell" by the majority of translators. The word *tartarus* was apparently quite common among many of the "classical Greek writers." It came from the beliefs of Greek mythology. In this belief it supposedly was "the lower part, or abyss of *hades*." I've written in some of my other books of the influence that Greek philosophy, and especially Plato, has had on Christianity. In this area it is the same. According to Plato's *Gorgias* regarding *tartarus* "souls are judged after death and the wicked received divine punishment." Not only was *tartarus* a place in the underworld, according to the Greeks, *Tartarus* was also a deity. Per the Greek poet Hesiod, in his *Theogony*, Tartarus was the third of the primordial deities, following after Chaos and Gaia.

2 PETER 2:4

As stated, *tartaroo* appears only one time in the New Testament, and that is in 2 Peter 2:4. Our English translation of this verse in the *King James Version* reads, "For if God spared not the angels that sinned, but cast them down to hell, and delivered them into chains of darkness, to be delivered unto judgment." Virtually all commentators say that since the word *tartaroo* only appears this one time we must look to see how the Greeks used it, and then most proceed an attempt at explaining Peter's comments with the Greek teaching in mind. That explanation, and the one most of us have been given, is that this verse is speaking of "fallen angels," or demons having been cast down into this particular area of the underworld, *Tartarus*. But, is that what Peter was talking about? Most of us never question the explanations we have been given, however, I believe it behooves us to look at the context here and see if that teaching fits with the rest of the Bible. (A quick note: The Bible **does not** support or teach that an archangel rebelled and became "satan" and that there were "fallen angels." For a detailed look at what the Bible does teach about these beings please obtain and read my book *AN EXPOSÉ OF THE ADVERSARY*, available from Amazon and other book sellers.)

A STUDY OF 2 PETER CHAPTER TWO

The disturbing verse for many is found in the second chapter of II Peter, verse four, "For if God spared not the angels that sinned, but cast them down to hell, and delivered them into chains of darkness, to be delivered unto judgement." I was always taught, and I find it is the teaching of the majority of Christian groups and churches, that this verse is speaking of "fallen angels" or demons. (See my note above.) Most often we don't question the teachings of the majority. We assume the teaching to be correct. I believe it behooves us to read this verse in context, to put the whole chapter together, and see exactly what the Apostle Peter was saying.

Let us begin with verse one, "But there were false prophets also among the people, even as there shall be false teachers among you, who privily shall bring in damnable heresies, even denying the Lord that bought them, and bring upon themselves swift destruction." Notice, Peter is telling us that there were, in times past, people who were false prophets. False prophets were and are those who give predictions that are incorrect, that do not come to pass. These individuals were among the people in times past **just as** there shall to be false teachers among us. False teachers, just like false prophets, will be teaching and predicting things that are not true, damnable heresies, Peter says. He says they will even deny the Messiah and will "bring on themselves swift destruction."

Continuing with verse two Peter says, "And many shall follow their pernicious ways; by reason of whom the way of truth shall be evil spoken of." Many, he says, will be taken in by those false teachers and will follow their "pernicious ways," the way that leads to destruction. Keep in mind that Peter is still speaking of people — false prophets, false teachers and the many who follow them.

Let us go on to verse three, "And through covetousness shall they with feigned words make merchandise of you: whose judgement now of a long time lingereth not, and their damnation slumbereth not." Peter tells us, as so commonly is the case, these false teachers try to make money and realize financial gain from those they are teaching and instructing. Adam Clarke defines "feigned words" as "counterfeit tales, false narration, pretended facts, lying miracles, fabulous legends." What they are saying is pleasant to listen to and sounds plausible but is in truth lies. Due to this they have brought themselves under the judgment and damnation of God, a time of correction.

ANGELS THAT SINNED

Now we come to verse four, "For if God spared not the angels that sinned, but cast them down to hell, and delivered them into chains of darkness, to be reserved unto judgement;" As stated above, I was always taught that this is referring to "fallen angels," but is it? Does Peter jump from speaking of men, false prophets, and false teachers, to talk of "fallen angels"? Well, it says "angels" doesn't it, and wasn't it the "fallen angels" that we were always told that sinned? Let us look at the Greek word translated into the English word "angels." It is #G32 in Strong's, *aggelos* or *angelos*. Although it is translated generally "angel" the primary definition and the valid translation used in several places is "a messenger, envoy, one who is sent." *Young's Literal Bible* translates this word in this very verse "messengers." Let us read it thus and see if the rest of the verse makes sense. "For if God spared not the messengers (those who were sent) that sinned (transgressed God's law), but cast them down to hell and delivered them into chains of darkness." As we mentioned earlier, the word translated "hell" in this verse is from a Greek word found nowhere else in the entirety of the Bible. It is #G5020 in Strong's, *tartaroo*, which we are told is from *tartaros*.

What does this word mean? As covered briefly above, almost all of the scholars tell us that since it is found only this one time in the Bible we have to look elsewhere for how it was used. Where we find it used is in Greek mythology. The Greeks believed Tartarus to be the "place of punishment in the lower world." I do not believe, nor do I think, that most Christians would believe that Peter is endorsing the nonsense of pagan mythology. If he did, then we would have to accept all of the absurdities that go along with it. However, many have accepted this teaching, not knowing where it came from. We do know that it is never taught or referred to in the Old Testament or anywhere else in the New Testament.

Peter appears to allude to the subject as though it was well-known and understood by his readers. Where is the story of individuals, or "fallen angels," being cast down to Tartarus recorded? As stated, it isn't in the scriptures. However, there was such a story in a book that was well known at the time of his writing, the Book of Enoch. (This book is not one that appears in the canon of scripture, the Bible.) It is from this apocryphal book that Peter seems to quote, or at least, refer. If he was doing this, did he sanction it as true, or did he, as many writers do, use it to illustrate and enforce his statements regarding the disobedient, the unrighteous, the false prophets being kept for later judgment? I believe, **if** he was referring to this story, it is nothing more than the way some writers might refer to the story of "the tortoise and the hare." They don't actually believe the story of a race between the two but use the Aesop fable to illustrate or make a point. However, I believe there is a much better understanding of what Peter was expressing in this passage. We'll look at that near the end of this chapter.

Though the account in the Book of Enoch does deal with sinning angels, which the Bible doesn't discuss at all, from the context of this entire chapter (as we will see more clearly as we go on) it is men that Peter is talking about. One writer makes the following comment, "Tartaros—this word occurs only once, in 2 Peter 2:4. A little Bible investigation will reveal that the angels or messengers, God's servants who rebelled, were Korah, Dathan and Abiram — Numbers 16:30-33. The earth opened and swallowed them up. The pit in verses 30 and 33 is *Sheol* in Hebrew — **the** *grave* — and it is there that they await judgment." I haven't studied this enough to be able to say that he is correct but I do believe it is plausible and it certainly makes more sense to me than to believe Peter is speaking of "fallen angels."

CHAINS OF DARKNESS

If we don't make the assumption that most make, that Peter is speaking of fallen angels, and continue to read in context, we can understand what he is saying. He is stating that these individuals are cast away from God's presence, literally into the earth, if it does happen to be Korah, Dathan and Abiram he is referring to. He says that they were delivered "unto chains of darkness." There was literal darkness in that pit but Strong's tells us that darkness is used metaphorically "of ignorance respecting divine things and human duties, and the accompanying ungodliness and immorality." A second definition states, "persons in whom darkness becomes visible and holds sway." God and His truth is Light. The opposite is darkness.

"Chains," as we read here, are not literal. It is rather an indication that these individuals are bound by this darkness, this blindness if you will, until, as the last part of the verse states, the time of judgment. They are "reserved," kept for the purpose of judgment, a time of correction. Many assume judgment is a time of destruction. God's judgment is to correct, with punishment as needed, to bring one to reconciliation.

Let us continue through this chapter and we will see more clearly that Peter has not jumped from his discussion of individual people (false prophets, etc.) to spirit beings. Verse five, "And spared not the old world, but saved Noah the eighth person, a preacher of righteousness, bringing in the flood upon the world of the ungodly;" Did you notice the same phrase used in verse 4, "And spared not"? Peter is still speaking of people, the old world, and speaks of Noah who was righteous. Noah is being contrasted to the ungodly, those outside of the "light" and in the "darkness."

In verse six Peter continues speaking of people who lived and acted contrary to God and His way of life. "And turning the cities of Sodom and Gomorrha into ashes condemned them with an over-throw, making them an ensample unto those that after should live ungodly;" Peter continues in verse seven to talk about people. "And delivered just Lot, vexed with the filthy conversation of the wicked;" The contrast continues to be between the righteous, the just, and the ungodly, those in darkness. Continuing to speak of Lot in verse eight Peter says, "(For that righteous man dwelling among them, in seeing and hearing, vexed his righteous soul from day to day with their unlawful deeds;)" His contrast between the righteous and the unrighteous continues.

Verse nine says, "The Lord knoweth how to deliver the godly out of temptations and to reserve the unjust unto the day of judgement to be punished;" Did you notice the wording in this verse, "to reserve ... unto the day of judgement," is almost identical to what we read in verse four, "reserved unto judgement." Verse nine is definitely speaking of people, as the context is making very clear, so also is verse four.

Let us continue reading with verse 10, "But chiefly them that walk after the flesh (not spirit) in the lust of uncleanness, and despise government. Presumptuous are they, self-willed, they are not afraid to speak evil of dignitaries." Peter is still talking about people, the ungodly, the unrighteous. Verse 11 says, "Whereas angels, which are greater in power and might, bring not railing accusation against them before the Lord." Does Peter now begin speaking of spirit beings, angels? Again the word is *angelos*, which can be just as properly translated "messengers." What "messengers" are greater in "power and might" than the ungodly, the unrighteous? Obviously those that are obeying and following God.

Verse 12 is quite plain that Peter is still speaking of people. "But these, as natural brute beasts, made to be taken and destroyed, speak evil of the things that they understand not; and shall utterly perish in their own corruption;" He says "these" still speaking of the ungodly and amplifying verse 11. He then refers to them as "natural brute beasts," akin to calling them nothing but animals. Continuing with verse 13, "And shall receive the reward of unrighteousness, as they that count it pleasure to riot in the day time. Spots they are and blemishes, sporting themselves with their own deceivings while they feast with you;" Peter is still speaking of the false teachers, the ungodly.

Verses 14 through 16, "Having eyes full of adultery, and that cannot cease from sin; beguiling unstable souls: an heart they have exercised with covetous practices; cursed children; Which have forsaken the right way, and are gone astray, following the way of Balaam the son of Bosor, who loved the wages of unrighteousness; But was rebuked for his iniquity; the dumb ass speaking with man's voice forbad the madness of the prophet." Peter hasn't varied from his theme. He is still talking of the ungodly, the unrighteous, the false prophets, the false teachers.

In verse 17 Peter starts out by saying, "These..." just as he began verse 12. The same "these." Let us go on, "These are wells without water, clouds that are carried with a tempest; to whom the mist of darkness is reserved for ever." In verse 12 he said "these, as natural brute beasts." Here in verse 17 he says, "These are wells without water," In both verses he is still speaking of men. Going back to verse four we read, "and delivered them into chains of darkness, to be reserved unto judgement." The wording here in verse 17 is similar, "to whom the mist of darkness is reserved for ever." But, doesn't "for ever" indicate for all eternity? No! The Greek is *aion* which is best translated age or ages. Peter is saying that these individuals have been "reserved," kept, in a state of spiritual darkness for the age, until the age or time of judgment.

Peter keeps speaking of these individuals. Verse 18 states, "For when they speak great swelling words of vanity, they allure through the lusts of the flesh, through much wantonness, those that were clean escaped from them who live in error." Verse 19 continues, "While they promise them liberty, they themselves are the servants of corruption; for of whom a man is overcome, of the same is he brought to bondage." He keeps right on speaking of these individuals that he first called false prophets and false teachers. Verse 20 says, "For if after they have escaped the pollutions of the world through the knowledge of the Lord and Saviour Jesus they are again entangled therein, and overcome, the latter end is worse with them than the beginning." He is still speaking of people. Notice verses 21 and

22, "For it had been better for them not to have known the way of righteousness, than, after they have known it, to turn from the holy commandment delivered unto them. But it is happened unto them according to the true proverb, The dog is turned to his own vomit again; and the sow that was washed to her wallowing in the mire."

The entire context of this chapter is the unrighteous, the ungodly, the false prophet, the false teacher, in contrast with the righteous. Peter repeatedly states in various ways that they have been placed into darkness, spiritual blindness, and kept there until the day, the time, the age of judgment. It is totally out of context to bring "fallen angels" into the discussion at all. Due to the translation given by those translating from the Greek and the incorrect assumptions and teachings of most of Christianity, we have failed to grasp and understand what Peter was telling us.

THE BOOK OF JUDE

We find an almost exact series of verses in the book of Jude. Jude is writing to those "sanctified by God the Father, and preserved in Jesus, and called:," verse one. He says in verse three that it was needful for him to write unto them and exhort them "that ye should earnestly contend for the faith which was once delivered unto the saints." In verse four he begins his discussion by saying, "For there are certain men." The context is men. He continues, "crept in unawares, who were before of old ordained to this condemnation, ungodly men." Much as Peter wrote, he is speaking of the ungodly, unrighteous men. In verse five he continues to speak of men, "having saved the people out of the land of Egypt, afterward destroyed them that believed not."

Now we come to verse six, which sounds almost like Peter's statement in II Peter 2:4, "And the angels which kept not their first estate, but left their own habitation, he hath reserved in everlasting chains under darkness unto the judgement of the great day." The word translated "angels" is again *aggelos* or *angelos* and can be accurately rendered "messenger." Notice how *Young's Literal Bible* translates this verse, "messengers also, those who did not keep their own principality, but did leave their proper dwelling, to a judgement of a great day, in bonds everlasting, under darkness He hath kept." See the above explanation of chains, judgment. But, one might ask, what about the "everlasting" chains? Doesn't that mean for all eternity? No!

The Greek word translated "everlasting" is *aidios*. I'd like to quote a section from a book that I would recommend that thoroughly discusses the subject of everlasting, eternal, forever, etc. as used in scripture. The book is entitled *The Greek Word AION— AIONIOS, Translated Everlasting—Eternal in the HOLY BIBLE, Shown to Denote Limited Duration* and was written by John Wesley Hanson, copyright 1875. Quoting from the Appendix of this book regarding the word *aidios:*

> "It is further admitted that the word is here used in the exact sense of *aionios*, as is seen in the succeeding verse: 'Even as Sodom and Gomorrah, and the cities about them in like manner, giving themselves over to fornication, and going after strange flesh, are set forth for an example, suffering the vengeance of *eternal* fire.' That is to say, the '*aidios*' chains in verse 6 are 'even as' durable as the '*aionion* fire' in verse 7. Which word modifies

the other? The construction of the language shows that the latter word limits the former. The *aidios* chains are even as the *aionion* fire. As if one should say 'I have been infinitely troubled, I have been vexed for an hour,' or 'He is an endless talker, he can talk five hours on a stretch.' Now while 'infinitely' and 'endless' convey the sense of unlimited, they are both limited by what follow, as *aidios*, eternal, is limited by *aionios*, indefinitely long."

Mr. Hanson also points out that the "everlasting" chains are limited by the fact it was to last only until "a judgment of a great day."

Just as we saw in 2 Peter 2, the context here in the book of Jude continues to speak of men. Verse six, the people of Sodom and Gomorrha. Verse eight speaks of "filthy dreamers." In verse nine Jude tells us that there had been a contention between Michael and the adversary about the body of Moses and Michael dared not bring a railing accusation. He continues the thought in verse 10 by saying, "But these (the people, individuals he has been speaking about) speak evil of those things which they know not:..." Verse 11 says they, these individuals, have gone the way of Cain, after the error of Balaam, and he says they "perished in the gainsaying of Core." Verse 12 continues, "These.." This is the same these, the people he has been discussing throughout the whole letter. He says they are spots, clouds without water, trees without fruit, and verse 13, raging waves of the sea, wandering stars. He says, "to whom is reserved the blackness of darkness (we have discussed "darkness" above) for ever. "Ever" is from the Greek *aion*, properly translated "age." (See the book referenced above for a very detailed and complete discussion.) Verse 14 says that Enoch prophesied of "these," the same these he has been discussing, unholy and unrighteous men. Verse 15 speaks of the judgment to be executed on the ungodly, the "these" he has been talking about. Verse 19 refers to verses 17 and 18 regarding the words which the apostles of Jesus had spoken regarding mockers in the last time that would walk after their own ungodly lusts. He says, verse 19, "These (the same these) be they...having not the Spirit."

Neither Peter nor Jude speak of angelic beings sinning but of unrighteous and ungodly men. Due to unfortunate translation and pagan beliefs that crept in, we have been taught error regarding these passages.

GRAMMAR IS THE ANSWER

To truly understand 2 Peter 2:4 we must take a grammar lesson. The ones who create lexicons (*Strong's, Thayer's, Liddell-Scott*) all tell us that the noun *Tartarus* does not occur in this verse but that the verb *tartaroo* does. Yet, they will give us a definition of *tartaroo*, which they tell us is a verb, as "cast down to hell." Let us look at that phrase closely, "Cast down" is an action word, a verb. "Hell," rendered for *Tartarus*, is a noun, "a person, place, or thing." What is that? How does a word that is a noun, which isn't in the original, come to be inserted and somehow made to be part of the verb, "to cast down"?

We have two words, *tartaroo* and *Tartarus*, which are similar in spelling and pronunciation, **but** which are unrelated, being combined, attempting to alter what Peter was stating. Let us read this verse again, without putting in the words "to hell," which comes from Greek *Tartarus*, originating in Greek mythology. "For if God spared not the angels that sinned, but cast them down, and delivered them into chains of darkness, to be reserved unto judgment." Peter **did not** need to add a noun to his verb, actually two verbs. Take notice. The verb is "cast down." "Them" is speaking of those the action is against. Peter also uses a second verb, "delivered," the Greek word *paradidomi*, Strong's number G3860. Among the number of ways this word is translated is "cast, entrust, commit, and deliver." Two verbs are being used, "cast down" and "delivered," both having much the same meaning. Now Peter supplies the noun he had in mind and wrote into this verse, "chains."

Not only is *Tartarus* not found in this verse, there is absolutely no need for it nor does Peter have a word from Greek mythology in mind. So, how did this come about? As discussed earlier, Greek philosophy and especially the teachings of Plato began to be incorporated into Christian teaching very shortly after the original apostles of Jesus were no longer on the scene. By the time Constantine "converted" to Christianity and declared it to be the official religion of the Roman empire, the belief in heaven as the reward of the saved and hell as the place of the wicked was already being taught. In his opening address to the Nicene Council (May through the end of July 325) Constantine made it quite clear what should be adopted as the official view of the new Roman Church regarding "eternal destiny." He sided decisively with Plato and the Alexandrian devotees, Clement and Origen.

A few years later (382 A. D.) Pope Damasus commissioned Jerome to translate the gospels into Latin, the official language of the Roman Church. Jerome went on to translate the entire Old Testament as well. Even at this early date he translated the Hebrew *sheol* and the Greek *hades* as the Latin word *inferno* (or variations based on forms, etc.) or "hell" in English. The English word "inferno," received from the Latin, is defined as "an intense fire" and is also shown to be "a place or state that suggests hell." The indications are that Jerome did not translate the rest of the New Testament, but that it was done by other anonymous translators. When they translated 2 Pet. 2:4 they used both "inferni" and "tartarum." The Latin reads, "*Si enim Deus angelis peccantibus non pepercit, sed rudentibus* **inferni** *detractos in* **tartarum** *tradidit cruciandos, in judicium reservari.*" (My emphasis.) Google Translate renders this into English as, "For if God spared not the angels that sinned, but cast them down to the depths of hell, and delivered them into Tartarus to be tormented, to be reserved unto judgment." Whether these anonymous translators added the word *Tartarus*, or they borrowed this from others that had added the word to Peter's writing is unknown. The rendering really doesn't come close to the Greek that Peter wrote.

We need to keep in mind that hundreds of years later the Bible was translated into English. The translators didn't rely just on the Hebrew and Greek scriptures **but** they depended quite heavily on the *Latin Vulgate*. In doing so they followed Jerome's and the other translators', lead in most instances as to the translation of *sheol* and *hades* **and** also the addition of *Tartarus* in 2 Peter 2:4. (We'll discuss the *Vulgate* a bit more in the next chapter.)

CHAPTER SEVEN

JEROME'S LATIN *VULGATE*

We touched upon Jerome's *Latin Vulgate* at the end of the last chapter. I believe it needs to be expanded upon a bit. Known generally as Jerome or "Saint Jerome," his full name was Eusebius Sohronius Hieronymus. He was born sometime between 342 and 347 in Stridon, Dalmatia. He died on September 30, 420, age 73-78, in Bethlehem, of Judea. His early education was begun at home but at about the age of 12 he went to Rome to study. His courses of study were grammar, rhetoric and philosophy. By the time he was about 20 years old he had completed his Roman education and was viewed as a serious scholar. He spent the next 20 years traveling, staying only short periods of time in any one location. He associated with a number of other scholars and writers. It was during these years that he spent approximately 2 years as a hermit in the desert. He learned Hebrew and studied Greek and a couple of other languages during these 20 years.

RETURN TO ROME

Following his 20 years of traveling, Jerome returned to Rome where he served as secretary to Pope Damasus, 382-385. Jerome was commissioned by Pope Damasus to produce a revised version of the four gospels in Latin. There had been many translations of the Bible into

Latin by individuals for use in their own communities. These various translations were known as the Old Latin or *Vetus Latina* and had accumulated piecemeal over a century or more. Jerome's work on the gospels was mainly a revision of the numerous Vetus Latina versions, not an entirely new translation. One would think that upon revising the gospels Jerome would continue with the rest of the New Testament, but that is not what he did. On his own initiative he extended his work to a revision and translation of the Hebrew scriptures, the Old Testament, which took 15 years of work. Just who the other individuals were that revised the rest of the New Testament is unknown. It is believed that most of the work had been accomplished by 410 AD. Over the next several hundred years there were other books added, referred to as Deuterocanonicals and non-canonicals. By the early 1500s numerous Catholic and Protestant biblical translations or revisions in Latin had appeared. Quite a number of theological disputes had arisen over the canonical status of many of the books. The Council of Trent (1545-1563) both finalized the biblical canon and re-endorsed the *Vulgate* among all of the Latin versions "to be held authentic."

The Vulgate was the source text used for many translations of the Bible into the vernacular languages. More than 2 centuries before the well known King James Version came into existence an Oxford professor and theologian named John Wycliff undertook the first-ever English translation of the Bible. The hand-printed "early version" of the *Wycliff Bible* first appeared in 1382, a literal translation of the *Latin Vulgate*. By 1395 this "early version" had been amended by Wycliff's friend John Purvey into a "later version." When the

King James Version came along it was built upon and came out of
the *Wycliff Bible*, especially the "early version."

THE VULGATE'S HELL

The Latin Vulgate, as it has come down to us, uses the Latin nouns
inferno, infernus, infernum, inferos, inferi, inferus, and *inferna* in
every place the Hebrew *sheol* and the Greek *hades* were used in the
Hebrew and Greek scriptures. In the *King James Version* most of us
are familiar with, there are 39 books in the Old Testament and 27 in
the New Testament. *The Vulgate*, as approved by the Roman church,
contains many more. However, if we compare only the books in the
KJV with the same *Vulgate* books we find a few interesting things.
In the KJV Old Testament the word *sheol* from the Hebrew is found
65 times and was translated grave 31 times, pit 3 times, and hell 31
times. 53 times in the *Vulgate* the nouns listed above, forms of *inferno,* are used, the words giving the connotation of "a huge fire that
is difficult to contain" and is applied to the hell that is taught. 11
verses that contained *sheol* had no equivalent word or were not even
in the translation. In one verse the Latin *mortis,* (death) is used. In
all of the 53 places the word *sheol* was translated, the Latin *inferno*
and its other forms were used. In the New Testament the Greek
hades was found 11 times. The KJV translated 10 of those times as
"hell" and one time as "grave." The *Vulgate* used *inferno* in its various forms in the same 10 verse the KJV used "hell." Where the KJV
used "grave," (1 Cor. 15:55) the *Vulgate* used the Latin *mors* meaning "death."

Earlier in this book we looked at the Greek word *gehenna,* from
the Hebrew *Ge-Hinnom,* the valley of Hinnom. In all 12 places this

word is found in the Greek New Testament the KJV renders it as "hell." *The Vulgate* actually transliterated this word as *gehennae*, however it has been adopted into Latin and used in the same way it came to be used in the KJV, "hell." Checking a Latin dictionary found on the internet 2 definitions are shown. The first says "from valley near Jerusalem where children were sacrificed to Moloch" and the second, "Hell."

As we covered earlier, John Wycliff produced an English language Bible almost 200 years before the King James Version came about. Even though he was knowledgeable in many languages, including Hebrew and Greek, his translation was almost exclusively a translation of the *Vulgate* and by all indications he translated the Latin *inferno* (and its numerous forms) and *gehenna* as "hell" in English. Of course, when the KJV was produced the *Wycliff* and the *Vulgate* were both used quite extensively. A couple of other things occurred along the way that solidified the use of "hell" and its concepts within the church. We'll look at those as we move forward.

Chapter Eight

Dante Alighieri's Divine Comedy

At the end of the last chapter I mentioned that there were a couple of other things that had major influence on the doctrine and teaching on "hell" within Christianity. The first one I want to briefly explore, without too much detail, is the fictional work of Durant di Alighiero degli Alighieri, most often referred to as Dante. He was an Italian poet, writer, and philosopher who lived from May 1265 to September 1321. He is mostly known for his poem, which has come to be considered one of the most important poems of the Middle Ages and the greatest literary work in the Italian language. He called it *Comesia*. Numerous manuscripts and commentaries on this work began to appear almost immediately after its completion. By the 16th century the word "divine" was added to the title and his work was treated like scripture. The imagery spawned by Dante's fertile imagination has been absorbed to varying degrees by Christians everywhere.

INFERNO

Dante's poem was composed of three sections, or canticles: *Inferno, Purgatorio, Paradiso*. Our brief examination here will deal only with the first section, *Inferno*. *Inferno* is a description of Dante's fictionalized journey that he took through "hell" himself, supposedly guided by the ancient Roman poet Virgil. I find it interesting to note the response found on the internet in answer to the question "What is Dante's Inferno based on?" The answer given was that "it is based on Catholic theology, and the Bible (although I don't see much of the Bible), as well as classical epic poems and mythology, such as the *Aeneid*, *The Iliad*, and *The Odyssey*." I have not read through all of this (and don't intend to do so) but did find and read a "full book summary." I find what Dante has put forth has absolutely nothing to do with scripture. He does not even credit God with this place labeled "inferno or hell." The characters he mentions, in addition to the one called Satan, are mythical beings and people from past ages.

His overactive imagination breaks "*inferno* or hell" into numerous sections or "circles." Many of these are further divided. As he supposedly moves from one circle to another he categorizes sins that progressively move from bad to worse, at least in his mind. God does not categorize sin. Sin, especially the sin nature we inherited from Adam, is all treated the same and is washed away by the blood of Jesus. Dante invents various tortures he somehow believes may be appropriate for the sins he envisions the individuals assigned to the various circles are guilty of. I don't wish to discuss all of these, but they include having hornets bite and worms lap their blood, individuals lying in mud and having to endure a rain of filth and excrement, some spending eternity in a river of boiling blood, and others trapped in a pit of vipers. There are more horrible torments that Dante dreamed up. If you know any of the Bible you know that none of these are found there, that these do not speak of the God of the Bible, the God who is **love**.

Dante's poem has contributed an immense amount of false teaching to a belief invented and taught by the Greek philosophers. I'd like to end this chapter with a quotation from the *Catholic Encyclopedia* article, *Dante Alighieri*.[18] "The power of the sacred poem in popularizing Catholic theology and Catholic philosophy, and rendering it acceptable, or at least intelligible to non-Catholics, is at the present day almost incalculable."

---

[18] https://www.newadvent.org/cathen/04628a.htm

CHAPTER NINE

JOHN MILTON'S
PARADISE LOST

A second powerful item that influenced the prominent view of "hell" was a work done in the 1600s. *Paradise Lost* is an "epic" poem written by John Milton, an English poet. He was born in 1608 and died in 1674. The first version of his poem was published in 1667. It contained ten books and was followed by a second version in 1674, which was arranged into twelve books. Milton went blind in 1652 and this work was written entirely through dictation. Multiple commentators have classified John Milton's poem, *Paradise Lost*, as a work of "Christian mythology." "Christian mythology" has been defined as "the body of myths associated with Christianity."

It becomes quite apparent, when doing an internet search for information on this work, that it is somewhat inspired by the Biblical account of Adam and Eve, the serpent, and prevalent teachings by "the church" and various church fathers and leading theologians. It is stated by many that while his poem may draw heavily on biblical texts and alludes to scripture, Milton introduces many interpretations and expansions that are not found in the Bible. Reviewing this work very briefly one soon finds details, dialogues, and characterizations that are not found in scripture. Many things reflect his own theological and political beliefs. One commentator states that this poem is "a work of artistic expression rather than a literal retelling of scripture." One individual pointed out that Milton was a poet, not a theologian, and as such "was free to use his imagination to create a compelling narrative."

Milton's Depiction of Hell

Milton put forth details, not found in scripture, regarding the adversary, Adam and Eve, and especially of "hell." He did draw some ideas and thoughts from some of his religious predecessors (including Dante) but much of what he portrayed was simply from his own imagination. He pictured "hell" as a place of utmost suffering, terrible horror, and excruciating terror. Here is a short quotation from one commentator on this work, Dr. Ashoke Kumar Agaewal:[19]

> "It is the 'infernal world' of horrors, a horrible dungeon burning like a huge furnace. Yet, from the burning flames comes no light as is needed to make the darkness visible. The medieval notion that the flames of hell give no light followed the idea that the damned are deprived of the sight of God who is light. Hell is a sorrowful place where 'rest can never dwell' and hope, which comes to all human beings, is totally absent. It is a murky land which has only doleful shades to droop and drown. Milton in this regard refers to Dante's concept in <u>Inferno</u>: 'abandon all hope, ye who enter this place.'"

Milton uses some very striking images, which he draws from various sources, to focus the reader's attention on fire. It appears that Milton's descriptions are very terrifying and he sought to infuse a

---

[19] https://www.jkcprl.ac.in › download

feeling of horror in the minds of his readers. He describes "hell" as a literal pool of fire that cannot be put out and with a darkness that one could actually see, or feel. Many feel that Milton did draw upon some religious predecessors to design his idea of hell, some, if not most, details are simply from his own imagination. Others have expressed that Milton was portraying "hell" as a place of fire, sulfurous fumes, and constant suffering.

Milton's Influence on Christianity

Sadly much, if not most, of what is believed by Christians comes from sources other than the Bible. Here is a quotation from an article titled *American Christianity and the Hell of Paradise Lost:*[20]

"It seems safe to say that most Americans know something about the concept of hell— that fiery place of torment that you go to if you're not up to snuff with St. Peter (or something like that). And while numerous religious perspectives conceive of something similar to the Christian conception of hell (think of Hades for the ancient Greeks), what many people don't realize is that the hell commonly conceived of by Americans isn't really based on Biblical portrayals of someplace called hell. Indeed, much of what we think about hell and its prince, Satan, comes not from any scriptural text, but instead from the epic poetry of John Milton."

---

[20] https://pursuingveritas.com/2015/02/26/american-christianity-and-the-hell-of-paradise-lost/

Later on in this same article the author, Jacob J. Prahlow, has this to say,:

> "...that almost nothing Milton has used to imagine Hell comes from a canonical source specifically describing Hell. The cultural consciousness of many American Christians concerning a description of Hell, in large part, comes to us through Milton's writing in *Paradise Lost.* While few would be able to point to Milton as a source of their perception of Hell, his work has undoubtedly shaped American Christianities conception of Hades."

A number of similar comments can be found when searching the various commentaries on Milton's poem. In an essay posted on the studycorgi website,[21] titled *Hell and Heaven in Milton's Paradise Lost Poem,* the author (not named) stated, "Overall, it can be concluded that the contributions of Milton are essential for the broad understanding of the concept of Hell." Near the end of the essay the author stated, regarding Milton's depiction of "hell," "It is still essential for the understanding of Hell and the various processes happening there."

Without spending more time, I believe we have presented enough to show that what most believe concerning "hell" comes from extra-biblical sources (such as Milton's poem and Dante's Inferno), from the fertile imaginations of men. A false teaching is embellished and becomes the widely accepted belief among those who should obtain doctrine from the Bible.

____

[21] studycorgi.com/hell-and-heaven-in-miltons-paradise-lost-poem/

CHAPTER TEN
DID JESUS GO TO HELL?

APOSTLE'S CREED

As one article found on the internet puts it, there is a tradition in historical Christianity that claims that Jesus descended into hell during the three days He was in the grave. Support for this widely held belief comes from the *Apostle's Creed*. Perhaps most don't know it, but the Apostles of Jesus didn't write the *Apostle's Creed*. It was rather a compilation of doctrines and beliefs that emerged from their teachings and the teachings of the early church leaders. It is believed to have originated in the 2nd century. The "creed," as most often recited by many today, contains the phrase "he descended into hell." This phrase was not in the earliest versions. It was first inserted by Tyrannius Rufinus, a Roman priest, writer, philosopher, and theologian, in 390 A.D. Most scholars point out that Rufinus, however, did **not** intend the phrase to mean that Christ descended into "hell." He simply meant that Christ was buried. There were at least five more versions of the "creed" after Rufinus, but none of them contained the expression "he descended into hell" until someone inserted it again in 650 A.D.

THE COMMON TEACHING

Due to the influence of the Greek philosophers the Hebrew *sheol* (which we discussed in CHAPTER TWO) meaning "the grave" had come to be defined as "the place of the dead" or "the place of departed souls/spirits." The Greek *hades* (discussed in CHAPTER THREE) with many added meanings had been used to translate *sheol.* The teaching, from Plato and the Greek philosophers, was that *sheol/hades* was a realm with two divisions. One was viewed as a place of blessing and the other a place of judgment. Both of these supposed abodes were called *hades.* According to many holding to this teaching, the abode of the saved was called "Abraham's bosom" or "paradise." Abraham's bosom was simply an expression signifying an intimate relationship. (Please see my book *THE RICH MAN AND LAZARUS – THE JEWS AND JESUS* for a more detailed explanation.) The teaching is that the unbelieving dead went to the cursed side or the lower region of *hades.* So, it is taught that Jesus, following His death, went to the blessed region of *sheol/hades* during those three days and "ripped its gates off the hinges, liberating Abraham, Isaac, Jacob, David, John the baptist, and the rest of the Old Testament saints." It is further taught that after His resurrection, Jesus ascended to heaven and bringing the ransomed dead with Him, so that now "paradise" is no longer down near the place of torment, but is up in the third heaven.

THE IMMORTALITY OF THE SOUL

For one to believe and accept the teachings that stem from the Greek belief that *hades is* the abode of the spirits of both the lost and the saved and in the belief that Jesus went to "hell" there must be "an immortal soul." Here is where we have a problem. The scriptures **do**

not teach that doctrine. The doctrine of the immortal soul also came to us from the Greek philosophers. Let me share with you a few quotations. The first one is taken from the doctrinal dissertation of Thomas Marshall Miller, Princeton University, 2015, titled *Plato's Doctrine of the Immortality of the Soul.* Dr. Miller states in the very first sentence in his abstract for the dissertation, "Plato's doctrine of the immortality of the soul is one of his most influential ideas, one adopted, developed, and criticized by philosophers and theologians from late antiquity to the early modern period." This next quote is taken from the *Encyclopedia Britannica*[22] article regarding the immortality of the soul. "But the idea of the soul as a mental entity, with intellectual and moral qualities, interacting with a physical organism but capable of continuing after its dissolution, derives in Western thought from Plato and entered into Judaism during the last century before the Common Era and thence into Christianity."

Here are a few more miscellaneous quotations from a number of comments found on the internet. "The concept of an immortal soul, while influential in later religious and philosophical traditions, likely originated in ancient Egypt and Babylon. The ancient Greeks, particularly Plato, adopted and popularized the idea." "The ancient Greeks, especially philosophers like Plato, significantly shaped the concept of the immortal soul." "While not explicitly stated in the Hebrew Bible (Old Testament) or the New Testament, the idea of an immortal soul gained traction in Jewish thought through contact with Greek philosophy, particularly Platonic thought. This concept

---

[22] https://www.britannica.com/topic/Christianity/The-immortality-of-the-soul

later played a significant role in Christian theology as well." One more, "Many of Plato's prognostications on the nature of the human soul may sound surprisingly familiar to the Christian reader who has never read a sentence of his dialogs. His views on the soul have had the noteworthy effect on the minds of great Christian thinkers, such as Origen, Saint Basil, and Tertullian, to name a few prominent examples. Many of these Christian writers were steeped in Greek philosophy prior to their conversion to Christ, making the acceptance of Plato's doctrines almost facile."

(For a more detailed study of an immortal soul please obtain and read my book *WHAT DOES THE BIBLE SAY ABOUT AN IMMORTAL SOUL?*)

UNDERSTANDING DEATH

When one looks at and understands the Bible's clear teaching on what death is the false doctrine of an immortal soul doesn't "have a leg to stand on." I have devoted an entire chapter, CHAPTER FIVE, to examining what the Bible reveals death to be. I'll give you just a few clear scriptures here and suggest you go back and review the whole chapter.

Psalm 146:4 "His breath goeth forth, **he returneth to his earth; in that very day his thought perish.**"

Ecc. 9:5 "For **the living know that they shall die**: but **the dead know not anything**, neither have they any more reward; for the memory of them is forgotten."

Jesus gave us a most powerful teaching on what death is, recorded for us in John chapter 11. (This is covered in detail back in

CHAPTER FIVE.) The account is about the death of His friend, Lazarus. Read with me verses 11-14:

"These things said he: and after that he saith unto them, Our friend **Lazarus sleepeth**; but I go, that I may awake him out of sleep. Then said his disciples, Lord, if he sleeps, he shall do well. Howbeit **Jesus spake of his death**: but they thought that he had spoken of taking of rest in sleep. Then said Jesus unto them plainly, **Lazarus is dead**."

From one end of the Bible to the other death is over and over again called "sleep." Sleep, as we all know from our own personal experience, is a state of unconsciousness to all that is happening around us. We are having no thoughts, we aren't planning anything — we aren't praising God — nor are we thinking of good or evil. Jesus says this is exactly what death is.

The scriptures are extremely clear. There is no consciousness or feeling in death. Man's soul does not live on as many try to claim. Just as people wake up from sleep, Jesus taught over and over again of a resurrection where all would "awake."

WHAT ABOUT THESE SCRIPTURES?

Before we close out this chapter I believe we need to look at a few scriptures that those who teach that Jesus went to "hell" oftentimes use in an attempt to give scriptural authority to the teaching. As we will see, these passages **do not** do so.

Acts 2:27 is a part of Peter's message on the day of Pentecost. Peter is quoting from Psalm 16:10, "Because thou wilt not leave my soul in hell, neither wilt thou suffer thine Holy One to see corruption." Although some would attempt to tell us that Jesus was in "hell" after He died, that is **not** what is being said. As has been pointed out numerous times, the Hebrew *sheol*, the word used in Psalm 16, simply meant the grave. Sadly the Greek *hades* which was used to translate the Hebrew *sheol* has accumulated a lot of false meaning. It too was used here in Acts to mean "the grave." A number of translations leave the word as *hades*. *The New International Version* (copyright 1973, 1978, and 1984) translated this verse clearly and correctly, "Because you will not abandon me to the grave, nor will you let your Holy One see decay." Sadly with their 2011 revision they moved away from that and now rather than "grave" render it "to the realm of the dead." If we are honest with the original meaning of *sheol* and *hades* it is clear what both David and Peter were telling us, that Jesus wasn't left in the tomb past the three days and three nights He said He would be there. And, He was there the whole time or else He lied and is not our savior.

Ephesians 4:9 and 10 have been used by some to show Jesus went to "hell." Let us look at these verses and see what Paul was saying. "(Now that he ascended, what is it but that he also descended first to the lower parts of the earth? He that descended is the same also that ascended up far above all heavens, that he might fill all things.)" At least in the 1984 copyrighted NIV the translation is better. Verse nine says, "What does 'he descended' mean except that he also descended to the lower earthly regions?" Several Bible commentators see "His descent" as His coming to earth as a man. Adam Clarke says about verse nine, "The meaning of the apostle appears to be this: The person who ascended is the Messiah, and his ascension plainly intimates his descension; that is, his incarnation, humiliation, death, and resurrection." John Gill says, "These words are a conclusion of Christ's descent from heaven, from his ascension thither; for had he not first descended from thence, it could not have been said of him that he ascended; for no man hath ascended to heaven but he that came down from heaven, John 3:13." These verses have absolutely nothing to say pertaining to Jesus going to "hell."

Jesus gave as His only sign He was the Messiah the "sign of Jonah." He said, Matt. 12:40, "so shall the Son of man be three days and three nights in the heart of the earth." The phrase "the heart of the earth" has been taken by some to mean "hell." He simply meant that He would be in the tomb, the grave, for those three days and three nights. Once again let us note what some commentators have to say. Albert Barnes says, "The Jews used the word 'heart' to denote the 'interior' of a thing, or to speak of being in a thing. It means, here, to be in the grave or sepulchre." John Gill's note on this verse has much the same to say, "That Christ means himself by the 'son of man,' there is no reason to doubt; and his being laid in a tomb, dug out of a rock, is sufficient to answer the phrase, 'the heart of the earth, ' in distinction from the surface of it." *Jamieson, Faucett, Brown Commentary* says, "The expression 'in the heart of the earth,' suggested by the expression of Jonah with respect to the sea, means simply the grave, but this considered as the most emphatic expression of real and total entombment." Matt. 12:40 does **not** support a teaching that Jesus "went to hell."

Spirits In Prison

The last passage we will look at is perhaps the one most often referred to when an attempt is made to show from scripture that Jesus went to "hell." The verses are found in 1 Peter 3, specifically 18, 19 and 20. We'll read them and then examine exactly what Peter is saying:

> "For Christ also hath once suffered for sins, the just for the unjust, that he might bring us to God, being put to death in the flesh, but quickened by the Spirit: By which also he went and preached unto the spirits in prison; Which sometimes were disobedient, when once the l ongsuffering of God waited in the days of Noah, while the ark was a preparing, wherein few, that is, eight souls were saved by water."

There are numerous teachings on these verses. There are many ideas as to just who "the spirits in prison" were. Some hold to the idea that angels married women, resulting in giants. (Gen. 6:1-2 is frequently used. We'll not go into this belief here.) The most common teaching supposedly drawn from these verses is that after Jesus' body was placed in the tomb He went to "hell" and "preached" to the Old Testament saints. Let us look at what Peter did say. In verse 18 he says "Christ also hath once suffered for sins, the just for the unjust, that he might bring us to God, being put to death in the flesh, but quickened by the Spirit:" He is telling us that Jesus lived a sinless life and yet suffered for the sins of all of mankind, the just for the unjust. He did this that He might bring us to God. Jesus, he says, was put to death and He was resurrected, quickened by the Holy

Spirit. Jesus died a physical death as all of us must do and He was raised to life by the Holy Spirit.

Let us continue with verse 19, "By which also he went and preached unto the spirits in prison;" "By which" refers back to "the Spirit," the final words of verse 18. It was by this same Spirit, the Holy Spirit, that the "spirits in prison" were preached to. As we continue into the next verse we receive more information.

1 Pet. 3:20 says, "Which sometimes were disobedient, when once the longsuffering of God waited in the days of Noah, while the ark was a preparing, wherein few, that is eight souls were saved by water." Over in the second book of Peter, 2 Pet. 2:5, we are told that Noah was a "preacher of righteousness." It was through Noah that the Holy Spirit of God preached to the people of Noah's day while the ark was being built by Noah and his sons. I want to draw our attention to a couple of verses that will help us understand. First let us read Jesus' words recorded for us in Luke 4:18-19, "The Spirit of the Lord is upon me, because he hath anointed me to preach the gospel to the poor; he hath sent me to heal the brokenhearted to preach deliverance to the captives, and recovering of sight to the blind, to set at liberty them that are bruised." This was a quotation from Isaiah 61:1-2. Let us read those verses. "The Spirit of the Lord God is upon me; because the LORD hath anointed me to preach good tidings unto the meek; he hath sent me to bind up the broken-hearted, to proclaim liberty to the captives, and the opening of the prison to them that are bound; To proclaim the acceptable year of the LORD, and the day of vengeance of our God; to comfort all that mourn;"

It seems clear that the "captives" in Luke and Isaiah, and the "prisoners" in 1 Peter are both referring to living people in bondage to sin, **not** disembodied spirits in *sheol/hades*. It is through Jesus that we all are freed from sin. John 8:32-36 states that we shall know the truth and the truth shall set us free. The people responded by saying they had never been in bondage, but Jesus said that whosoever commits sin is in bondage, a servant of sin. He said if He, the Son, should set us free we shall be free indeed. Clearly all are in bondage to, or prisoners, of sin. Yet we have been set free by the Son of God. This was the message preached through Noah by the Holy Spirit when the ark was being built.

But, you may be asking, "Doesn't it say spirits?" I've stated in many of my writings that commentaries are the words of men, not scripture. However, much that is found is good and explains difficulties in translation and the like. I do believe Adam Clarke's commentary on 1 Pet. 3:19 is quite good and gives us understanding. His comments are quite lengthy, so I'm only quoting a portion. The following is taken directly from his commentary. (You may want to obtain his commentary and read the rest of what he covers.)

"**Unto the spirits in prison** — The inhabitants of the antediluvian world, who, having been disobedient, and convicted of the most flagrant transgressions against God, were sentenced by his just law to destruction. But their punishment was delayed to see if they would repent; and the long-suffering of God waited one hundred and twenty years, which were granted to them for this purpose; during which time, as criminals tried and convicted, they are represented as being in prison — detained under the arrest of Divine justice, which waited either for their repentance or the expiration of the respite, that the punishment pronounced might be inflicted. This I have long believed to be the sense of this difficult passage, and no other that I have seen is so consistent with the whole scope of the place. That the Spirit of God did strive with, convict, and reprove the antediluvians, is evident from Gen_6:3 : My Spirit shall not always strive with man, forasmuch as he is flesh; yet his days shall be one hundred and twenty years. And it was by this Spirit that Noah became a preacher of righteousness, and condemned that ungodly world, Heb_11:7, who would not believe till wrath — Divine punishment, came upon them to the uttermost. The word πνευμασι, spirits, is supposed to render this view of the subject improbable, because this must mean disembodied spirits; but this certainly does not follow, for the spirits of just men made perfect, Heb_12:23, certainly means righteous men, and men still in t he Church militant; and the Father of spirits, Heb_12:9, means men still in the body; and the God of the spirits of all flesh, Num_16:22; Num_27:16, means men not in a disembodied state.”

One other thing that Dr. Clarke pointed out was a clearer translation of the passage, referring to the Spirit, “by which also he went and preached unto the spirits in prison.” He shows that from older manuscripts the rendering would have been “by which he came spiritually, and preached to them that were in prison.” Properly understood these verses penned by Peter have nothing to do with evil spirits or with Jesus descending into “hell” during the time He was in the grave.

Conclusion

When we look at what the Bible plainly teaches and we turn from the philosophy of the Greeks, the answer to our original question, "Did Jesus Go To Hell?" is plain. **No**, He did not go to an imagined location where "spirits" of dead saints from the Old Testament awaited. **No,** didn't go anywhere during the three days and three nights He was in the tomb. He was dead. He died. He had explained just a short time before His death that death was equated with sleep. He was dead, asleep, waiting to be awakened, resurrected. And, exactly three days and three nights from the time He was placed in the tomb He awoke from that sleep, resurrected. He remained there in that grave for the entire time, the entire 72 hours. As I have said, **if** He didn't His word was not good and we don't have a savior.

CHAPTER ELEVEN

LET US RECAP

"HELL" DEVELOPED

This book has been written specifically for those of us of the "Christian religion." However, most of the other major religions of the world have a belief in a "hell" of some type. Although there are various beliefs among Christians, it has been believed by most that the doctrine is taught by the Bible.

We have made our best attempt to show you, the reader, that this horrible doctrine does **not** come from the pages of the Holy Bible but from the "wise" of the world, the philosophers who, apart from God, have developed these ideas. The apostle Paul's words to the church at Rome come to mind. Notice Romans 1:22, "Professing themselves to be wise, they became fools." "Wise" is translated from the Greek word *sophos.* This was a title that the "wise men" of old attached to themselves. Later they began to use the word *philosophos,* or philosopher, signifying one who loves wisdom. Their wisdom was not the wisdom of God. James 3:15 speaks of this kind of wisdom, "This wisdom descendeth not from above, but is earthy, sensual, devilish." Let us look at the rest of Rom. 1:22, "they became fools." This phrase is translated from the Greek word *moraino,* which means "to become a moron or simpleton."

We looked at the fact that "hell" was never in the Hebrew scriptures. The Hebrew word *sheol*, meaning "the grave," was used. *Sheol* was a proper name and should never have been translated. But, it was, and that translation should have been "the grave." By the time our English language Bibles came about, a Germanic word, *hel*, meaning "to cover" or "to conceal" was selected and used to translate *sheol*. (Never mind that Hel was the name of the Scandinavian queen of the underworld.) Along the line the "wise" began to come up with various ideas. Perhaps **the** idea that caused all these other ideas to be formulated was that of the "immortal soul." **If** one had an "immortal soul" there had to be some place for it to go when death occurred. *Sheol* began to be, not just the grave, but a place where these souls went. And, boy oh boy, did the imaginations run wild. All kinds of beliefs developed leading to much of what people are taught in our churches, never mind that none of it came from the Bible.

As we followed the evolution of the words that came to be translated "hell" and carried with them the concepts arrived at by the "wise men," the philosophers, we found these ideas permeating the entire culture. The Greeks came up with a word, *hades*, that to them conveyed all of their ideas and beliefs. However, when it was used to translate the Hebrew *sheol*, totally wrong thoughts, ideas, and doctrines were promulgated. These false ideas and concepts were very pervasive, entering into the teaching of the early believers, especially after the original apostles were no longer on the scene. Those who came to be viewed as the "church fathers" immersed themselves in Greek philosophy and accepted and taught what they learned, becoming, as Paul said, "morons and simpletons." Jesus and the apostles, especially Paul, gave warning after warning that false teachers would enter into the church, bringing damnable heresies. This teaching of an ever burning place of torment was among the greatest.

Over time the concept of "hell" became further "developed" with the imaginations of men such as Dante and John Milton. In their overactive imaginations they put forth concepts regarding the supposed tortures that awaited those they envisioned going to this "hell." Although their poems were clearly fiction, they soon took on an equality with Holy scripture. Dante referred to his poem as a "comedy" but soon others added "divine" to the title. It is known by all today as "*The Divine Comedy*." Most believers in the doctrine of "hell" don't even realize most of their beliefs come from these fictional sources, not the Bible. Those early "fathers" of the church soon found scriptural passages they could twist to appear to support their beliefs. It appears that most theologians and Bible teachers have accepted the explanations these men came up with and have never **really** studied the Bible to see what it truly has to say.

I won't belabor what we have already presented in the previous 10 chapters. However, I'd like to ask a few questions that perhaps you have never considered. When I wrote my first book, *God's Bestseller Make It Real In Your Life*, a handbook on how to study the Bible, I pointed out that one of the most important things we need to do is ask questions. Have we ever asked ourselves, or others, if this doctrine of "hell" as generally taught and understood depicts the God we say we worship? The Bible says that God **is love**, not that **He loves**. We are told that "He so loved the world, that He gave His only begotten Son" (John 3:16). Jesus said He came to reveal the Father. He taught us to pray "Our Father." God is the perfect Father, the perfect parent. How can we even entertain such a thought that

He would take any of the children He loves and consign them to an eternity of torture? He apparently, as seen by many, requires more of us than He requires of Himself. Through Jesus He said that we should forgive others "seventy times seven." But, this "hell" doctrine would indicate that if one fails to accept Jesus before he dies or perhaps never even heard the name of Jesus, God would not forgive but would cast this individual into such a place as described by the "wise" for all eternity?

It is easy to see why some have little or no interest in Christianity when the One they are told "loves them" would treat His own children, the ones He purports to love, in such a horrendous way. Thankfully this terrible doctrine has no basis in truth. Thankfully we **do** have a heavenly Father that truly loves each and every one of His children. Thankfully He has a plan in place to bring each and every person who has ever been born, or will be born, to reconciliation and salvation. (For a thorough under-standing of that plan obtain and read my book *The Ultimate Reconciliation And Salvation Of All*, available on Amazon and other booksellers.)

Praise God He is true **love**. Praise God He never conceived of such an abominable doctrine. Praise God you have had revealed to you the truth. Praise God you and I can give Him praise and glory that He isn't as He has been wrongfully depicted. Praise God "hell," as taught and believed by so many, is just one of the devil's deceptions!

About The Author

Garry D. Pifer has been a reader and student of the Bible for over sixty years. In the mid-nineties he embarked on a much more diligent study. He wrote most of his studies in article form, many being put onto the internet and some published in an independent journal. In 2020 he authored *God's Bestseller: Make It Real In Your Life!* This book is a handbook giving a step by step guide to studying the Bible, giving the reader the benefit of what he had learned over 25 years. Led by the Holy Spirit he has donated over 2400 copies to prisons and jails across America.

Garry and his wife, Connie, have been married for sixty-one years. They are the parents of four grown children. They have eleven grandchildren and six great-grandchildren. They currently reside in South-Central Kentucky.

Garry may be contacted by writing to him at P. O. Box 131, Edmonton, KY 42129 or by E-mail: gdpifer@scrtc.com

Other Books
By Garry D. Pifer

God's Bestseller:
Make It Real in Your Life!

Many have often wanted to understand the Bible but just thought it was a very confusing and closed book. In this conversational and straightforward book, Garry D. Pifer presents a step by step guide that will take you from a lack of understanding and a place of confusion to an opening up of what God has hidden **for** you, not from you. This book will give you direction in your search of the Scriptures. You will find priceless riches and treasures of great price. Read this book and learn how to find what has been concealed.

Shadows Of Jesus in The Exodus

Most have not grasped the numerous shadows in the Egyptian Passover and of the exodus of the Israelites from Egypt that have their fulfillment in the final days of Jesus, His death, burial, and resurrection. This study takes you through the many details of the exodus, establishing the timeline of the events, and moves on to the New Testament where the same timeline is revealed in the events of Jesus' final days and hours. Surprisingly you will find that many of the events did not occur on the days most Christians have been told that they happened. For an exciting study get and read *Shadows of Jesus in the Exodus.*

THE HISTORY OF TITHING: WHERE ARE WE TODAY?

The doctrine of tithing 10% of one's income is taught in almost every church. Where and when did tithing begin, what was tithed upon, and to whom did it belong? Are we as new covenant believers under a command to tithe? For the complete history of tithing and whether it applies to you and me please obtain and read *The History of Tithing: Where Are We Today?*

WHY AREN'T CHRISTIANS THE HEALTHIEST PEOPLE ON EARTH?

It seems that most Christians believe that God exists and that He is all powerful. Most believe that He is able to heal all sicknesses and diseases, but they are not sure that He will. Some believe that He brings sickness upon us to teach us lessons. Almost everyone appears to believe that God has given us the medical system for our health and healing and many aren't sure that divine healing is happening today. *Why Aren't Christians the Healthiest People on Earth?* looks at these beliefs and more. Garry D. Pifer will share his journey in the study of divine healing, looking at what the Bible reveals. What he discovered in his study may be totally contrary to what you have been taught and have believed from childhood. This challenging and thought provoking book can be read in one or two sittings but may lead to weeks and months of study and examination on your part.

An Exposé of The Adversary

An Exposé of the Adversary looks at who the devil is, what his purpose is, where he came from, and the part he plays in our lives. *An Exposé of the Adversary* unveils and exposes the many lies he has foisted off on mankind, including the lie that Lucifer and Satan are his names. *An Expose' of the Adversary* dismantles his biggest lie, that he was an archangel that rebelled against God. Prepare to have the beliefs of a lifetime erased by *An Exposé of the Adversary*.

The Ultimate Reconciliation and Salvation of All

The Bible declares over and over again that God is unwilling for any to perish and that it is His will that all be saved. However, due to many commonly taught, and believed, doctrines of the Church most have been unable to grasp this most glorious and wonderful truth. Garry D. Pifer takes the reader through many scriptural passages showing the truth concerning these doctrines and then looks at what the Bible declares God's will and purpose to be, and the ultimate destiny of each and every individual that has ever had life. One may find what is presented challenging but also the most wonderful good news ever revealed.

Do Christians "Go to Heaven" When They Die?

90% of Christians believe that when they die they will go to heaven. They have heard this from infancy. Yet, if they are honest, they will have to admit that they have never heard a complete sermon or Bible study taking them from "Genesis to maps" to prove or disprove it. In *DO CHRISTIANS "GO TO HEAVEN" WHEN THEY DIE?*

Garry D. Pifer will lead you in such a study and will also look at history to answer that question. You may be surprised at the answer.

THE RICH MAN AND LAZARUS — THE JEWS AND JESUS

The common teaching regarding the story of Lazarus and the rich man is that it contrasts "hell" and "Abraham's bosom," said to be heaven. However, when examined in detail, Garry D. Pifer shows that this is not the story Jesus was presenting at all. Mr. Pifer reveals from scripture who these individuals are and what Jesus was truly teaching. In *The Rich Man and Lazarus – the Jews and Jesus* you will find that there is much more to the story than you have probably seen.

WHAT DOES THE BIBLE SAY ABOUT AN IMMORTAL SOUL?

According to recent surveys approximately 95% of American Christians believe they possess a soul that survives after the death of their bodies. A belief in an immortal soul has been extant in most major religions, Christian and non-Christian alike, for hundreds and thousands of years. Where did this doctrine come from, the Bible or elsewhere? What does the Bible say about the "soul?" Since many major doctrines, such as heaven and hell, are built on the foundational belief in an immortal soul, we really need to get the answer to our question, what does the Bible say about an immortal soul?

These books are available from Amazon
and other major booksellers.